D1737954

POLICEWORK

POLICEWORK

The Need for a Noble Character

Rickey D. Lashley

Foreword by Stan Stojkovic

Westport, Connecticut
London

Library of Congress Cataloging-in-Publication Data

Lashley, Rickey D.
    Policework : the need for a noble character / Rickey D. Lashley;
  foreword by Stan Stojkovic
      p.   cm.
  Includes bibliographical references (p.) and index.
  ISBN 0–275–95013–1 (alk. paper)
    1. Police ethics—United States. 2. Law enforcement—United
States—Moral and ethical aspects. I. Title.
HV7924.L37 1995
174′.93632—dc20   94–32921

British Library Cataloguing in Publication Data is available.

Library of Congress Catalog Card Number: 94–32921
ISBN: 0–275–95013–1

First published in 1995

Praeger Publishers, 88 Post Road West, Westport, CT 06881
An imprint of Greenwood Publishing Group, Inc.

Printed in the United States of America

The paper used in this book complies with the
Permanent Paper Standard issued by the National
Information Standards Organization (Z39.48–1984).

10 9 8 7 6 5 4 3 2 1

Over the course of my career in law enforcement I have served closely with scores of peace officers and have encountered hundreds. Along the way I have known a number of them whom I could only seek to emulate, for I could never exceed the standard they set. People who epitomize humility and dedication, they never seek to draw attention to themselves but shine brightly as examples of what it takes to do the job. And so this book is dedicated to the likes of Officer Kenneth Nieman, Detective Jess Bickle, and Officer Arthur Koch, people possessed of a quiet nobility-people of character.

Contents

Figures

Foreword

This book is about frustration. Much of the frustration is felt by criminal justice officials, politicians, and the general public. Their frustration can be traced to the perceived inadequacies of the criminal justice system in dealing with crime and the tragedy it produces. This frustration is felt when large formal bureaucracies–such as the police–are largely ineffectual in addressing crime and meeting the basic needs of the community. At the most basic level, this means to protect and serve the public in such a way that crime is controlled on the one hand, while on the other hand, do it in such a way that democracy is preserved.

It is the tension between these two competing interests that the history of American policing can be understood. In <u>POLICEWORK: The Need for a Noble Character</u> Rickey D. Lashley tries to examine why current attempts to confront crime in America are doomed to failure. He highlights what sociologist Egon Bittner noted over twenty years ago that the police role in America is confounded when there is a societal expectation that coercive force be employed in certain situations while being sensitive to the fact that a democracy deplores the expression of such non-negotiable force. The perennial problem, therefore, for the police administrator is to employ the coercive powers of the state without trampling on the constitution and laws that the police organization is sworn to protect.

Essentially, the answer in America has been the bureaucratization of police systems. The bureaucratic model has been touted as the most efficient and effective way to organize large numbers of people toward the completion of goals. Whether this is true or not has been the query of analysts for decades. Discussions on clarity of goals, goal ambiguity, and goal uncertainty have predominated among critics. These antagonists have argued that for the most part public organizations lack clarity of purpose, and that it would be undemocratic to seek maximum bureaucratic efficiency and goal certainty in public organizations, since their very nature is to reach out and reflect diversity of opinion and thought on how the organization in question should function. Such is the case for police systems in America.

Lacking a clear and unambiguous mandate, police organizations are bound to flounder and drift. What Lashley does is document this process, beginning with a discussion on the need for a reconceptualization of the police role given the futile attempts of addressing crime (in particular, the drug war) currently employed by police and concluding with ideas on how crime in the future might be more successfully addressed. His effort is no small endeavor. By using his own experiences, he is able to show why current initiatives to confront crime are headed for failure, but his analysis suggests more than limitations to the bureaucratic approach to policing. In addition, he argues that the police, the criminal justice system, politicians, and the community live under a false set of ideas and assumptions on how crime can be reduced in society. His most vociferous attack is against the police bureaucrat.

Lashley presents a view of the contemporary police official as indifferent, largely ignorant about the causes of crime, and most of all, only concerned about narrow turf interests and measures of police production that are worthless in relation to the real crime problem. Such a picture is unflattering and critical, yet Lashley paints this picture based on his many years of experience as a police officer and undercover drug agent. His realism is both refreshing and frightening. His call for reform in the ways police do business are not new, but what is different about his approach is his appeal to a sense of justice and character in police work.

Similar to other accounts of police work, such as Serpico, Target Blue and Prince of the City, Lashley presents realism and also asks us to reconceptualize the idea of the police. In addition to the standard arguments of adding more resources to improve police work, Lashley examines the limitations of the traditional paramilitary model in police organizations. Adding more to the same structures would be counterproductive. He argues that this traditional model only stifles the ordinary street cop and engenders a system whereby meaningless statistics become the goal of the organization with very little concern for actual crime reduction. Moreover, the "good cop" becomes the cynical cop and the police administrator ultimately settles for the role of a politician and professional bureaucrat. Such a system is untenable and will never be able to confront crime in an effective way.

What POLICEWORK offers the reader is a non-traditional view of the police organization. It is critical, yet hopeful; it is cynical, yet realistic; it is dogmatic, yet visionary. In the final analysis, Lashley offers us a challenge to rethink the nature of police work. The traditional approach to crime is not working and will not work. The "war" metaphor will only go so far, until a disgruntled public demands more. Lashley is asking for more from police; he seeks a noble character for police work. Whether you agree or disagree with his ideas and recommendations, it is essential that you continue to ask how American policing can effectively confront crime while adhering to the principles of a democracy. Lashley has begun to address this question. Egon Bittner would be proud.

Stan Stojkovic
University of Wisconsin-Milwaukee
Milwuakee, Wisconsin

Introduction: The Last Chapter

Entering the field of policework is akin to entering matrimony or parenthood. It serves to define one's identity and is a life choice producing psychological and emotional bonds rivaling those found within the family. It is the vocation of the proverbial artist, and leaving it is painful to the soul. But there are some things that one simply must face: the death of one's parents, the inevitability of old age, the rejection of a lost love, and the limitations of one's intellect or athleticism. So it was with my career-it was at an end. It had run its course.

It makes no sense that a man's proudest achievements would lead to his own disillusionment without the understanding that it was all for naught–hollow victories and perversions of the charge of justice. I had witnessed the murder of my ideals in my own lifetime, and we have all been robbed of justice for the sake of an unholy ruse. Jeffrey Reiman puts it the best when he notes that the American criminal justice system is like a "carnival mirror," serving to distort the image of the society it is designed to protect. We peer into the laws of our government and into the activity of our police, searching for an accurate reflection of the condition of our times. Instead, we are presented with a reality that is refracted through the vested interests of those in power, a truth distorted by far too many of the politcal appointees who head our police departments.

I know what it is like to race through the night in pursuit of a gunman who only minutes before shot another human being in the street. And I know the horror of an all too abrupt an end to that chase, with flames rising out of the engine compartment of my sqaud car, my partner's skull smashed by a broken window strut. I have watched men die the most violent of deaths, and I have been forced to fight for my own life. All of this and more have I experienced in my career as a peace officer, and I might still be doing it today if I thought it made sense. But it does not.

It came to a climax one dark night during a tactical narcotics raid on a group of houses in an inner city neighborhood. I can close my eyes and still see it. It was drizzling and chilly on the night of the Jones Street raid. I remember the cold cutting through the cloth of my raid jacket and seeping under my body armor as I emerged from my squad car outside the Public Safety Building. Scores of officers were involved in a combined effort by both the Racine Police Department and the Metro Drug Unit. I was a member of the latter, a counter-drug task force based in southeastern Wisconsin.

We assembled for the raid after dark. At the Safety Building, a large newspaper delivery truck had been parked inside the fire department garage, so as to be out of public view. It was an odd sight, the orange and white newspaper truck sitting among the bright red fire engines and brilliantly painted ambulances. An even stranger sight was dozens of peace officers decked out in full riot gear climbing into the back of a vehicle normally intended to transport stacks of newspapers.

The compartment went dark when the sergeant pulled down the overhead door and we drove out of the garage. Someone kicked on a streamlight; the beam reflected off the ceiling of the truck and onto the faces of the officers who were packed in about me. They had a controlled expression, anxious and tense about what lay ahead, and calm in the knowledge that we had been through this before and all should go right so long as each one did his or her job.

We lumbered through the city, riding the floor of the delivery truck like the deck of a ship as it swayed and bucked on its way to the raid location. Several officers kept their "handhelds" to their ears, listening for instructions as we approached. Finally, the delivery truck came to a halt.

Almost immediately the overhead door was shoved upward and we began to stream out, jumping onto the wet pavement and dispersing to our preassigned buildings. As luck would have it, I struck a metal post with my leg as I jumped, and as I landed on the street, my knee buckled in pain. There is little time in the middle of a raid to attend to a bump or a strain, however, and I half-hobbled and half-ran up the front steps of the address my team was assigned to hit.

The door was breached in seconds by the ram team, and we poured into the foyer like so many ants into a nest. Inside, the team would split; one group had already begun to spread throughout the lower level of the home. I started up the staircase and called over my shoulder for cover. I was breathing hard by now, and sweat was beginning to soak into my clothes. Noises could be heard from the bedrooms, and I realized there was someone upstairs. Upon reaching the top landing, I swung quickly across it, bringing my 9mm to bear as I did so.

There, in the sights of my pistol, was a group of children, frozen in terror at the sight of me.

I jerked the muzzle of my weapon away from its target, and with the sound of my heart pounding in my ears, I did my best to sound calm, reassuring them that all would be ok. The children ranged in age from about three to just about twelve. As the initial shock of our entry passed, the younger ones began to cry. I asked the older two to stay with the toddlers and keep them calm and together in one room while we searched the house.

By now one might expect that it was the sight of these children in my gun sights, like a bullseye on a target, that brings back the memory of this raid so vividly, but it is not. This had happened on raids before. Rather, it is a recollection of the scene occurring outside the house that has never faded.

Like so many of the homes we had raided over the years, this one was filled with squalor. Garbage littered the floors, and the children appeared not to have bathed for a week. The only food that was visible was rotting on the stove and counter tops in one of the filthiest kitchens I had ever seen. The smell was horrendous. I had to get some air before I lost my dinner on the living room floor.

In a hurry to reach the front porch, I bumped the door open quickly with the heel of my hand. The night air hit me like a breeze off Lake Michigan, and as I lifted my head to take a deep breath, I was met with one of the strangest visions I have ever seen. Backlit sharply by the porch lights of the houses across the street stood the surreal image of a SWAT team member in a black mask and wearing the gray urban camouflage of a tactical officer's uniform. Resting on his hip and jutting upward on a angle to his body was a military submachine gun, the eerie glint of a streetlight playing across the surface of its receivers. It was the image of a storm trooper, the specter of the power of the state perverted to an ignoble cause.

Across the way stood others like him, uniformed in black and gray, machine guns and pistols at the ready, securing the street from movement as would a garrison in time of martial law. It was unholy to see. It was un-nerving to recognize. We had come to this at last, and I wanted no part of it anymore.

Part I

THE NEED FOR A CHAMPION

1

The Need for a Noble Character

The modern police officer has been referred to as the blue knight, invoking the image of King Arthur's court of warrior peacekeepers. Certainly the imagery is there. The glint of metal from both the uniform of the police officer and the armor of the knight, and the common aspect of the badge and the coat of arms, carry over the romanticism from the earlier age to ours. In the fantasy of Arthur's reign, however, more important than outward decoration were qualities of character–of the heart. The legend hinged upon the nobleness of Arthur and of the men who swore allegiance to him. Courage, honor, loyalty, and a love for peace formed the substance of Camelot's magic. When the kingdom's monarch and knights held true to themselves and to the cause of peace and justice, its magic won out over that of evil. Only when the nobles lost sight of their duty and sense of honor could the dark forces prevail. In this, even more than in its imagery, the legend parallels today's reality because the importance of truth runs constant. There is a need for the noble character today; an urgency for virtue in all its forms. Still alive is the threat of the world of darkness once banished by the courage and magic of Camelot. The citizenry is still in peril and the knights of the faith are still their hope for justice.

That virtue is the key to peace is a long-standing belief. That peace–or order if you prefer–is in jeopardy is true, in that it has always been so. Virtue and decadence oppose each other, and battles are won and lost in an ongoing conflict. It seems from my perspective, however, that virtue is now under siege; it is locked within its walls, its knights at its parapets. Ground has been lost; ideals have not been advanced. We have not kept sight of duty and honor but have become complacent and looked away. The cost is an assault upon peace, security, and prosperity.

Whether or not virtue is indeed more threatened today than previously is not the critical question in any event. What is significant is that the ideals of honor and duty are difficult to attain. This is not to say that we have become decadent or that there is no one of integrity in law enforcement. It is to state that honor and duty must ever and more vigorously be pursued if peace officers are to achieve a quality so magical in its character as to approach the fantasy of Camelot. To the people of long ago, when the legend of Arthur was fostered, an armored knight whose heart and hand were pledged to a king such as Arthur epitomized a virtue so powerful in its potential that it could only be regarded as magical. A knight of the Round Table represented justice, and justice is indeed enchantment in that it nurtures harmony. Peace officers are in that sense knighted, and no less today than long ago is their charge of justice magical.

Justice, then, is the key to peace, and in their role as peacekeepers, law officers must accomplish fairness–not merely enforce statutes. Dealing in the intangible commodities of law, ethics, and morality, they must balance each with the other, using ideals as standards of measurement. Justice cannot be fixed within one or the other of these, as will be evident, but must be gleaned from their myriad aspects. Such an endeavor demands that officers stay true to their conscience and use their intellect, for, like it or not, they are arbiters as well as constables–the consequences of their decisions to act or not to act, or to act in a particular way, make this so. A police officer must practice a philosophy, not merely follow procedures. Morality–the heart, if you will–is inextricably a facet of law enforcement, and a police officer's character is the key to his or her success.

Moral values, then, play a large role in order maintenance, superseding mere procedure. To fully understand why this is so, the concept of values must be examined. Once the influence our values have on us is understood, the answer will be apparent.

A value is a belief about the relative importance or desirability of a particular behavior, goal, status, or quality. To attach importance to truthfulness, fame, and contentment is to hold values. Each of us structures such beliefs within a hierarchy of values,[1] some taking precedence over others. One might value education, but providing the family income may be a more important concern and will supersede if a conflict between the two occurs. Values, then, can be thought of as moral judgments about behavior.[2] They affect our decisions about how we will act.

Policing is therefore critically dependent upon our values, decision making being one of the salient features of order maintenance and often amounting to a process of weighing the relative importance of various factors that apply. In other words, much of what the police do is the result of value judgments. This is perhaps best made clear through the following examples:

A twelve-year-old is caught stealing an inexpensive toy by a department store clerk. The child has no prior police record. An officer is called to the scene and must make a disposition of the matter.

Immediately, values impose on the process. Arrest will stigmatize the child; the officer may see this as harsh. Shoplifting is a serious economic crime in terms of total loss; the officer may feel compelled to arrest. Processing an arrest of a juvenile will take hours; the officer may feel it a waste of his or her time. The store manager may be upset and want the child prosecuted; the police officer may feel that staying on good terms with the business community is important to his or her work. Obviously, these factors are critically tied to values, so, depending on the orientation of the particular officer, differing ways of handling this case will be decided on.

Police decisions involving value judgment also take the form of administrative policy. The types of activities that police agencies will concentrate their efforts on depend on values:

The chief of a municipal police department operates his or her agency with limited resources. The chief is faced with more demands on the departmental budget of man-hours and equipment than are available and must allocate them as he or she sees fit. Here again, "as the chief sees fit" translates into "according to the chief's values."

If winning the approval of the powers that be in the community is high in the chief's system of values, he or she will concentrate on looking good on paper. Statistics will be stressed, the chief demanding arrest whenever possible. Report writing will become an end in itself. Collecting copious files of needless reports, as this executive's officers will view them, will be a priority. In short, the agency will lose sight of its legitimate goals of order maintenance and community service, adopting instead a policy of looking efficient.

Alternatively, if the chief places a high value on reducing crime, effort will be skewed differently. Report writing will be simplified whenever possible, to conserve man-hours for street work. Statistics will be viewed as an aid–not as a goal–and arrest treated as an option to be used where appropriate. Here the direction of the department is toward bringing the resources it has to their fullest potential in order maintenance.

Whether on the level of the individual police officer or the organization, values and moral judgments are intrinsic to the police process and cannot be separated from the decisions and policies of law enforcement and its professionals. As the examples offered above have illustrated, an officer's or administrator's system of values will preordain how he or she will act.

Morality is, therefore, inescapably part of a police officer's role. It imposes on the process of law enforcement and cannot be discounted or ignored. It is a reality that each officer must learn to cope with and use to accomplish the positive. It will surface in his or her own actions, and will be encountered in the form of policy. The officer will feel its presence viscerally as it makes itself apparent through the emotions.

Each time a patrol officer decides whether to arrest a violator or to issue a warning, he or she will have an impact on the stability of the community. Also, whether an administrator elects to emphasize image or push for effectiveness will either reduce or elevate the quality of life of the citizens that commander is obligated to serve. These statements are so obvious they seem trite, yet they point to the most crucial factor of police decision making:

character. The only true standard with which to weigh such choices is justice—it must be the primary goal. An arrest should be made when it is just to do so, not to rack up points with the department. Resources should be used to protect the community, not the departmental image. Such decisions take character—a sense of honor. Crime and injustice are no less a threat now, in the real world, then they were in legendary Camelot. Duty and honor are likewise no less magical today than in the age of Arthur. To fulfill his or her sworn duty to protect the public, the officer must do more than acknowledge the obvious as being so; he or she must adhere to those principles that will bring it about. No less today than in Camelot, the heart is inextricably a part of the administration of justice.

NOTES

1. Richard A. Kalish, *The Psychology of Human Behavior* (Berkeley, CA 1973), 340-342.

2. Peter L. Berger and Brigitte Berger, *Sociology: A Biographical Approach*, (New York, 1972), 335.

2

Justice as a Scam

By priority, if you list the goals of criminal justice, the alleviation of crime and public disorder will stand primary. Who the criminals are and the causes of disorder are not as obvious. Our system of justice, like a misadjusted camera, is focused incorrectly; its perspective is narrowed. Not that the technician behind the lens is clumsy or misdirected–he or she is right on target in relation to the script. The story line is simply a bad one. Justice is skewed, and deliberately so. Police activity and that of the courts follow just such a script, and they and the audience have been duped. Much as a producer earns ratings by dressing an old plot in a new facade, those who determine our system of justice carry on an insidious deception. A much sharper focus must be obtained and a far wider angle of view must be sought if the truly big picture is to be seen.

Justice is a scam in that it misses the mark, striking instead a convenient scapegoat.[1] The thousands of criminals we have locked up in prisons and assigned to probation officers function as decoys, distracting us from the actual conspirators behind disorder. Street crime is the result of an intricate chain of causation, and criminality is rooted much deeper within the basic characteristics of our society. Order maintenance is the stated goal, yet social disorder on an alarming scale is the reality that persists. We must probe past the superficial "causes" of crime and societal breakdown if we are to uncover the true cause-and-effect mechanisms behind them; and since crime, simply stated, is a breakdown of social control, our system of social control will become our starting point.

CULTURE AND SOCIAL CONTROL

Culture is the sum of human adaptation, encompassing the accumulated knowledge and behaviors used in daily living. It delineates the accepted ways in which we deal with our environment and with each other, and regulates human activity-as is evidenced by the fact that each of us expects that others will act in accordance with it. It is, then, a system of social control, and society is culture in action (or the application of culture).

Within our society a system of interrelated processes and institutions functions to perpetuate human culture through time, maintain consistency through self-regulation, and enforce compliance with certain norms through the use of specific controls. Through such processes as socialization and social stratification, and such institutions as religion, education, and the family, culture is passed from one generation to the next (with some modifications). Because of this, society has continuity. A great deal of normative conduct is self-regulating and, as a result, culture has consistency in these areas. The concept of tradition is an example. Certain patterns of behavior-especially imposed norms-require specific controls or enforcement in order to be maintained; hence the need for such things as traffic tickets and civil suits. These three factors (self-perpetuation, self-regulation, and specific controls) work together to maintain an integrated, functioning society, though not perfectly so.

Human culture is the solution that Homo sapiens has arrived at in answer to the struggle of life in its environment. It patterns our lives by providing functional behaviors that make participating in society possible. Children receive the content of their parents' culture through socialization, and it is via this process that people "learn to become members of their society and culture."[2]

Later, as the child moves into the larger roles of student, worker, and community member, new learning must take place. New experiences are interpreted through the past learning of primary socialization, building on those underpinnings more complex technical skills and expanded attitudes and belief systems. As the individual passes through adolescence and into adulthood, new roles and new learning are experienced. He or she will learn to be a professional or a fiancee`, a parent, a retiree. New roles and new socialization occur throughout life in an ongoing process. This ongoing "posttoddler" learning is known as secondary socialization.

And there are times when there is a need even to resocialize an individual confronted with a stark change in cultural settings. An extreme example of this would be an Asian farmer emmigrating to urban America. Such a person is faced with learning a new language, a new job skill, and a new lifestyle. As we will see later in the chapter, such conditions can exist for persons without their ever leaving their country-or hometown!

As is evident, the socialization process is complex, involving a large variety of people and institutions. It is a lifelong process, and its later states are dependent on earlier ones for success. In this way society can be an ongoing enterprise and does not have to be reinvented with each generation. The cost of this advantage, however, is that our lives are subject to control and direction from birth on.

Along with human culture come the realities of such concepts as social class and differential access (the fact that the wealthy or members of the dominant majority have greater access to such institutions as the courts and government bureaucracies). Factors such as these combine to ensure that the status quo will be maintained; that there will be laborers to labor and entrepreneurs to organize; that there will be voters to pay taxes and lawmakers to levy them; and that those in power accrue the higher benefits of our society while those without power work to supply them.[3] The existence of social class regulates such things as the relative numbers of persons in the trades as opposed to the professions, and the relevance of social status is that it is capable of controlling how many of us will be allowed the luxuries of an economy endowed with only so much to go around.

NARROWING THE FOCUS

Why the lesson in social science? The answer, simply put, is "Criminal justice is social science applied." One cannot accurately view crime as strictly a legal issue. It is also one of economics, religion, philosophy, psychology, and sociology. Theft, after all, is another means of distributing wealth–the very definition of economics. Battery certainly violates the commandments of God. Criminal misconduct most assuredly falls within the boundaries of ethics, a subdivision of philosophy. The fundamental legal requirement of intent pulls criminal justice within the purview of psychology. An entire subdivision of sociology, that of criminology, is devoted to the study of crime. All considered, we would be remiss not to include these disciplines in our considerations.

The intent of exposing the reader to social science material is a modest one indeed, despite its import. It is only to begin the student of criminal justice upon a path of investigation into the myriad factors that must be appreciated if one is to understand crime and crime control. We still do not do justice here to each of the disciplines cited, let alone those unnamed. It is hoped, however, that an orientation of thought will be achieved that is eclectic in the study of law enforcement.

We are primarily interested, of course, in criminal justice, and our focus now that we have a base of information–will narrow to the specifics of that topic. It is important to know why such a system is needed and why crimes occur: in particular, why street crime is so common and why the system of legal controls fails to eradicate it. We will, in the pages to follow, apply what we have learned to specific points in an effort to understand these broader issues.

SPECIFIC ISSUES

I earlier called crime a breakdown in social control. There are many reasons why such breakdowns occur. For example, a youth raised in the ghetto does not learn the same values as a youth in middle America. But if the young man from the ghetto is to achieve success in America (the elusive American dream), he must live his adult life under the same requirements as a middle class boy. As we saw, the socialization process prepares children for adulthood, and adult learning builds on this. For a middle-class boy this works. He learns skills of the middle-class world and does well in the job market, marriage, and so on. For the ghetto boy the same is not true. He is raised with different skills: to work odd jobs if he can and, if he can't, to work the street; to be a companion, not a husband; and to be a client of the state, not a full-fledged citizen.[4] For such children to go mainstream as adults requires resocialization (a sharp break with past culture and taking on of an entirely new one). Without ever changing his address, the young adult enters a foreign world and is buffeted by the effects of a cultural shock. Many cannot withstand this especially in the face of poverty, illiteracy, and prejudice. As a result they continue to build behavior on the learning of their childhood and not the new environment. In this sense ghetto culture is a success in that it perpetuates itself-little other opportunity exists.

There are underlying factors, some of which are alluded to above, that serve to support the promulgation of a ghetto class, just as there are supports for maintaining the middle class. In a certain sense crime is both a breakdown of social control *and* a by-product of it. Society generates crime.

The maintenance of social classes is functional. Promoting a lower class is a means of resource conservation, for example. Maintenance of a middle class is necessary for economic incentive. Having the two in conflict is functional in the sense that it enables an upper class to escape close scrutiny by those of lesser rank. A power structure forms out of all of these and other relationships one that regulates the larger economic and social systems of society. In other words, class society is one scheme of social control.[5]

The unfortunate consequence of such a scheme, however, is the generation of chronic criminal conduct. Poverty, ignorance, and abuse inspire a dim view of the concept of legal ownership, a lack of understanding of the need for public order, and a disinterest in the pain of others. The criminal behavior resulting from such attitudes is readily visible to the public and provides a convenient set of reasons to scapegoat the poor and ethnic people of our society as the *cause* of crime, obscuring the perspective that they are merely more *susceptible* to criminal tendency. As a result, each feeds the other in a perpetual negative relationship. They perpetuate each other. Beyond this, opportunity is provided-out of the confused, disorganized condition of the mass of citizens-for the wealthy class to support its voracious need for money and all it can buy. At the same time each class can feel justified in its disdain for and abuse or use of the other for its own ends. The result, of course, is that we all suffer to one degree or another from the consequences of crime.

NOTES

1. Jeffrey Reiman, *The Rich Get Richer and the Poor Get Prison* (New York, 1979), 17.

2. For the bulk of the material on socialization I have drawn heavily on Carol A. B. Warren, *Sociology: Change and Continuity* (Homewood, IL, 1977), 267-283.

3. This is not to state that there is some central, upper-class conspiracy acting to regulate class exploitation through a covert orchestration. Forces arise in society that result from attitudes held by those in power and those without power that seem to each to be moral and supportable. A rich entreprenuer might be a devout Christian adhering to the Protestant work   ethic-perhaps rationalizing away the need to aid the poor by making tax-deductible contributions to his church. He might not see beyond the fallacy of his materialism. A lower-class worker might abstain from voting or from running for alderman, contending that government is a tool of the rich, and in so doing forfeit his or her right to political power. These sets of attitude and action combine to creat a force-a theme of power-that works to support and maintain a class society. And so it goes.

4. Please do not take these to be literal, unwavering absolutes. Not every ghetto family rears its children in this manner, just as not every middle class family is turning out all-Americans. We are dealing in preponderances here-degree. Tendencies arise in the two communities and should not be ignored. There is a basis for the difference.

5. See note 3.

3

A Question of Ethics: Misplaced Priorities

We have come to be aware that the police officer represents an ideal: justice. And it is upon this ideal that peace and order must rest. Thus, peace officers underpin society, and without a just police force any community is doomed to fall short of its potential.

Beyond this we have observed that there are sociopolitical forces that distort justice and impede society. Criminal justice can be perverted to less than noble ends. So long as the knights of Camelot held true to their ideals, justice did prevail; only when they lost sight of their duty did evil come to the kingdom. That magic is the same today. So long as the law enforcement officer holds true to the cause of justice, his or her actions can only be of assistance to the citizens the officer serves. Only when the police fail to adhere to standards of ethics and duty will they obstruct the cause of justice they are sworn to serve. This being so, how can the justice system come to be an enormous scam? How can such perversions be eliminated? One very constructive means by which to attack these problems is to treat them as a question of misplaced priorities.

Let us examine this issue by discussing how police departments react to misconduct on the part of the officers they employ. A great deal is made of the violation of accepting gratuities.[1] Not accepting gratuities is, in principle, a good policy. However, it is interesting to note that more in the way of official reaction is likely to come of an officer taking a free cup of coffee and a doughnut than of a commander accepting a complimentary membership in an athletic club. The same is the case with other matters of discipline. Dereliction of duty is one. An officer who fails to remain awake during the entire third shift and is caught can expect days off without pay. Yet a police administrator who elects to send himself or herself to a weeklong technical seminar (rather than the subordinate who will be expected to perform the function for which the training is intended) will not receive even a reprimand from the chief. This second example is quite telling as regards the issue of misplaced priorities because it speaks to the practice, common to police administrators, of offering scapegoats in response to the public cry for clean government while perverting the budgets and resources under their direction to their own private ends.

Junkets are common in government generally, and policework is no exception. They result in the waste of enormous amounts of tax money every year. Beyond this, they divert budget intended to enhance the technical skills of the officers who work the street and of the technicians who support them. A classic example is that of the out-of-state specialty school that provides the latest in police technology or techniques. Doubtless there will be some member of the department who is assigned to criminal intelligence analysis or to illicit drug interdiction and who is in need of technical training to become competent or to update his or her skills within the specialty. It has been my experience that such schools are often attended by a command-rank officer who enrolls in the program so as to "become familiar with an area of expertise being used within his or her command." Upon the officer's return, he or she "fully briefs and directs" the hapless subordinate whose job it is to conduct intelligence operations or drug interdiction. Such technicians sometimes find that the extent of their training consists of the command officer's tossing the handouts or texts provided by the training school into the lap of the individual who must actually apply the information or operate the equipment.

Such use of public funds is reprehensible, and it undercuts the mission of the law enforcement agencies that are intended to protect the public. Interestingly, many of the problems and failures of policing can be traced to similar perversions of police priorities. Why, for example, are the police so concerned with petty violations and not, it seems, as intensely concerned about violent crime? A huge percentage of the resources budgeted for law enforcement are utilized against minor infractions of law. Examination of the activity sheets (used to guide and measure activity in the field) reveals that many categories are specified in the realm of traffic enforcement and not so many in the area of crime prevention. Likewise, review of the inmate records of a county jail will reveal that persons convicted of driving with a revoked license serve minimum-mandatory, multimonth sentences while persons convicted of battery and burglary often receive only cursory thirty-to-ninety day sentences or probation. Why would such a distorted condition exist within the system of justice in this country?

The answer once again is misplaced priorities. It is difficult to apprehend burglars and even more difficult to rehabilitate them. At the same time it is easy to catch a driver with a revoked license. It is also easy to justify punishing such a person. After all, there is no defense against an allegation of driving while one's license is revoked. Either the officer saw the offender driving or the officer did not. It is cut and dried. There is no need for a plea bargain. Burglars, on the other hand, have an advantage. Such offenders can often mount a defense. A trial is more likely to result from a burglary allegation than from driving whith a revoked license. Juries, with all their inherent human frailties, will become involved. Time, money, and risk of acquittal stare the prosecutor in the face. It is much easier to strike a deal.

The actual priority in the case of the topsy-turvy justice outlined in the paragraph above is that of production. The system will crank out successful prosecutions (plea bargains, if need be) and will *look good on paper* (a common theme in this book) above all else. The prosecutors are busy looking good, grinding out numbers instead of combating crime in the street. So it is with police agencies. It is easy to count traffic tickets or service calls, but it is not so easy to measure the prevention of assaults or the inhibition of burglaries. The focus is on numbers, not effectiveness.

And what does this indicate overall about the priorities of law enforcement agencies? The paramount objective of a police department is survival. It is, after all, a bureaucracy, and it has long been established that the first order of business of a bureaucracy is survival.[2] This should serve as a strong hint to those who run municipal and state government as to how to influence the priorities of the police agencies within their respective cities and states–make survival *contingent on acquiescence to the true needs of the community* rather than on some placebo or symbol. Myths and symbols abound in police agencies. They are adept at image maintenance through manipulating such symbols as "community policing" and promulgating such myths as "proactive patrol strategies."[3] Too often, police agencies engage in public relations rather than in policework. Think again the next time you see a "new and progressive" federally funded traffic control program announced with great fanfare in the local news media. Look hard at proposals to enhance patrol effectiveness via an increase in the size of the uniform division. Demand instead, from the administration of the police department, a reduction in burglaries and violent assaults. Make budget contingent on a realignment of resources within the department aimed at increased field interviews with suspicious persons in residential neighborhoods at night. Make it a top priority of the police to patrol back alleys instead of metered parking areas. For police departments are like other bureaucracies. They will, by and large, do whatever it takes to survive, and if collecting statistics and revenue are the priorities that they are presented with, those are the ones that will be served.

It must be conceded, however, that the last sentence ignores the fact that not all police administrators are willing to engage in the gamesmanship that so often precludes the more noble goals of policework from taking the fore. Police commanders can make a difference. So can their subordinates in the field. They will do so only under pressure, however. Merchants, alderpersons, professional people of influence, and others will pressure these officials to cater to their interests. Parking turnover will matter to merchants, checking important persons' homes while they are on vacation to alderpersons, and keeping the riffraff off the streets of downtown will be dear to most professionals whose shingles hang above the sidewalks.

Police commanders and officers in the street can indeed make a difference, in that they can avoid becoming indoctrinated by politics to the point that they completely buy into the agenda that selfish but powerful people seek to promote. For example, a police professional should always realize that law enforcement should never be seen as a revenue collection agency. Maintaining this perspective will prevent a commander from designing policy to devote resources to that end. I have heard from the lips of high level administrators as recently as 1992 that they consider it a responsibilty of the patrol officer to write the maximum possible number of traffic citations so as to ensure adequate revenue to justify the maintenance or expansion of manpower levels. It stands to reason that running radar-in such a department's jurisdiction-will take up a large percentage of patrol hours. This being the case, it is doubtful that a very large number of field interview stops will be conducted (they do not produce much revenue, after all). Once the hierarchy of a police department accepts a petty agenda as the only agenda for its officers, it will have diverted the agency from its more noble goals of safe streets and secure homes. Certainly an administrator must at times compromise in order to survive, but he or she should never lose sight of the higher calling of law enforcement.

How do chiefs of police and other ranking police officials fall prey to such petty thinking and buy into such perversions of the mission of policing? In the same fashion that the patrol officer accepts a free meal at the local coffee shop or gets a "great deal" on a new car. Allegiances are bought by those who need influence to further their own goals. A car dealership quite naturally desires the contract for the police department fleet of squad cars. The athletic club may be looking for strict enforcement of the parking regulations in front of its building. Others may simply wish to be a part of the "in" crowd or the power structure. Powerful people have an affinity for each other, as is well known. And to quote Sam Rayburn, "If you want to get along, go along."[4] We do indeed live in a pluralistic society, filled with social classes and interest groups that do not share the same ideals and goals. That is why the police official, be he or she a chief or a patrol officer, must always rely on a single standard against which to weigh the conflicting demands for service and enforcement. The obvious choice is to measure them against the yardstick of justice. And the easiest means to do this is to build the mission of the department and the policies that emanate from it on the basis of a just community.

It would seem that I wax philosophic and lack practical substance at this point. How are we to determine this standard of justice? What form will such a mission will take? Well, it is here that, surprisingly, the answer is most obvious-perhaps too obvious to be readily apparent. Policework abounds with ready made accounts of mission and purpose. The Law Enforcement Code of Ethics, mottos such as "Veritas" and "Protect and Serve," state constitutions, and state and local statutes abound with such guidance. Yet the human animal is the king of rationalization. We can convince ourselves of almost anything. We can, for instance, tell patrol officers that they will get three days' suspension for drinking a free cup of coffee, yet regard a no–cost lifetime membership to the health club as a well deserved perk.

I have devoted precious little ink to the issues of police corruption in the traditional sense. Many competent books and essays address the topic well. I recommend reading of some of them. The law enforcement student or professional would do well to read Lawrence W. Sherman's "Becoming Bent: Moral Careers of Corrupt Policemen,"[5] which illustrates just how some officers come to accept bribes and even commit burglaries. One should also read the works of other writers, including Michael Feldberg's, "Gratuities, Corruption, and the Democratic Ethos of Policing: The Case of the Free Cup of Coffee."[6] These issues are, however, less insidious than the politics of policework and its corruption of the philosophy of law enforcement. Because of the subtlety of this latter point, I consider it a more crucial concern for this text. And it is also because the issue of politics and philosophy is so subtle and yet so critical that the next chapter is devoted to one such example, A-MEG.

NOTES

1.   Howard Cohen and Michael Feldberg, *Ethics for Law Enforcement Officers* (Boston, 1983), 31.

2.   Carol A. B. Warren, *Sociology: Change and Continuity* (Homewood, IL, 1977), 168.

3.   Charles Perrow, *Complex Organizations* (New York, 1986), 271.

4.   Tip O'Neill, *Man of the House* (New York, 1987), 140.

5.   Lawrence W. Sherman, "Becoming Bent: Moral Careers of Corrupt Policemen," in *Moral Issues in Policework*, ed. Frederick A. Elliston and Michael Feldberg (Totowa, NJ, 1985), 253-265.

6.   Michael Feldberg, "Gratuities, Corruption, and the Democratic Ethos of Policing: The Case of the Free Cup of Coffee," in *Moral Issues in Policework*, ed Frederick A. Elliston and Michael Feldberg (Totowa, NJ, 1988), 267-276.

4

A-MEG

A-MEG[1] is a pseudonym for an actual metropolitan enforcement group that operates somewhere in the Midwest. It is a countywide, multijurisdictional task force with the main responsibility for drug investigations within that county. A-MEG resulted from a federal grant program designed to encourage local and state law enforcement agencies to consolidate resources in the area of drug enforcement. In the late 1980s a great deal of federal and state matching funds were appropriated to a coalition of municipalities within the boundaries of a suburban county we will refer to as the County. Eight of the nineteen municipalities combined resources to establish A-MEG: the County, the larger of two cities (we will call it C-City), and six smaller municipalities. Three of the eight communities contributed sworn peace officers to serve as investigators for the unit, as well as equipment and budget. These were the County, C-City, and a township we will refer to as T-Town. The remainder of the municipalities contributed funding, use of facilities, and liaison support.

The coalition had ambitious plans for the newly established enforcement unit. The changes outlined in the preceding paragraph constituted major structural and budgetary innovations. It was hoped that consolidation would overcome the obstacle of jurisdictional boundaries via the mechanism of countywide deputization of personnel. Also, since every investigator reported to the same commander, coordination of their efforts was to be simplified. No longer would an investigation wend its way to the town or city line, only to end like a bridge to nowhere. Jurisdiction would be coordinated.

Operational command was to be centralized via the consolidation of personnel under one unit commander. Personnel matters such as payroll and discipline were to continue under the contracts and policies of the parent organizations.

Resources would be centrally administered, and C-City was designated as the municipality that would administer all grant monies. Parent agencies would be responsible for issuing payroll and benefits to their own personnel; the C-City finance department would administer the operational budget of A-MEG.

Communications also would be centralized, with the expectation that consolidation of personnel under one roof and command would automatically result in better communication between parent agencies. Staff meetings, a central intelligence file, interagency liaisons, the coalition board of directors, and similar mechanisms were instituted for the express purpose of improving communication and information flow.

A key to effectiveness of the new agency was believed to be the proper coordination of specialists in complex team investigations. Expectations were high as a result of the belief that upper-level drug traffickers would be susceptible to well-orchestrated historical conspiracy investigations (a complex, labor-intensive, long-term approach), sting operations, long-term undercover operations, and other techniques that had not been practicable under the old fragmented system. Highly specialized and tightly coordinated professional investigators were to be nurtured and put to use. Surprisingly, however, specialization efforts somehow came to be a fragmentary influence on A-MEG.

As we proceed, we will observe how well the people involved in creating and operating A-MEG were able to implement the processes we have listed. The ambitions of the founders of A-MEG were considerable and complicated. They sought to achieve consolidation of personnel and other resources without surrendering political oversight via a large-scale coalition and a complex organizational design. Unfortunately, the resulting organization fell far short of its goals.

ORGANIZATIONAL DESIGN

Traditionally, law enforcement agencies utilize the Weberian bureaucracy to structure their organizations. The Weberian design is one that has been written about extensively and is vividly described in Walter F. Baber's book *Organizing the Future*.[2] Baber outlines the essential characteristics of Weber's model as follows:

1. Create a hierarchy of authority;
2. Establish a system of impersonal rules;
3. Keep permanent, written records;
4. Create a division of labor and job specialization;
5. Maintain permanent offices to endure changes in personnel.[3]

The organizational structure put in place to support these principles is pyramidal in shape with orders flowing down from the top and feedback flowing up from the line. An illustration of this is Figure 4.1:

FIGURE 4.1
The Bureaucratic Pyramid

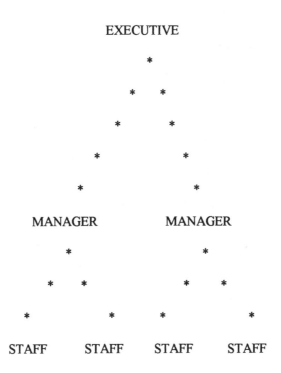

Such a design serves to support the type of processes that the A-MEG implementers sought for their organization. Coordination is achieved by the hierarchical structure, its vertical authority and specialized divisions making this possible. Centralized command is also well served by the fact that directives flow downward from the executive to the line. Resources are allocated in a systematic way as well. Communication is certainly centralized, following the same vertical channels as command and feedback. And task specialization is a hallmark of the classic bureaucracy by virtue of its use of subdivisions. It might appear that the traditional style of police organization is just what is needed by A-MEG.

The designers of A-MEG did not choose to structure the new narcotics task force after the fashion of a traditional police bureaucracy, however. Instead, they chose the organizational plan outlined in Figure 4.2.

FIGURE 4.2
The Structure of A-MEG

REVIEW BOARD * * * Advisory Board

        *

        *

        *

EXECUTIVE LIAISON

        *

        *

        *

COMMANDER   CCPD/CSD/TTPD

        *   *

        *   *

        *   *

        *   *

LINE INVESTIGATORS

The Review Board is to set policy and provide *joint political oversight*[4] of the program. It consists of the administrative heads of each of the three police agencies that contributed personnel to the department. The Advisory Board consists of the police chiefs of the eight participating communities. The commander holds the authority over day-to-day operations of the unit, and the line investigators perform the actual fieldwork. The role of the executive liaison is somewhat nebulous. One might conclude that he is the embodiment of the collective executive authority of the members of the Review Board yet in practice, his authority is often fragmented. The functional managers (C-City Police, County Sheriff, and T-Town Police) lie outside the primary chain of command. They are out of the loop in terms of operations and are concerned with functional issues such as payroll and employee benefits only.

This is quite a departure from the traditional police agency in terms of organizational design. It succeeds in centralizing authority, but operational command and functional administration have been split. There are written rules and regulations, but they are of a dual nature. Permanent written records exist within the program, in that A-MEG utilizes police reports, computer intelligence files, and similar in-house recordkeeping, but personnel records are maintained by the individual parent agencies and there are certain breakdowns in documentation. The effort to specialize is under way, but it is done on an ad hoc basis, with the commander assigning areas of responsibility to the various investigators. No formal plan is in place to develop trained personnel for the new job classifications.

Still, both the implementers and the unit personnel were optimistic concerning the potential for success at the outset of the program, and they remained so throughout the early years of A-MEG. It was felt that the problems of dual administration and multijurisdictional authority would be worked out. The consensus was that so long as everyone was willing to pull together and operational command was centralized, the unit could make remarkable progress.

WERE THE PROCESSES REALIZED?

Expectations concerning A-MEG were that the several governments involved could form a coalition to bring about the formation of a metropolitan enforcement group and that they could create a governing board to oversee it. This arrangement is significant in that the chief executives of the respective agencies consolidated their authority. But how does this executive authority of A-MEG act in an integrated fashion? Here the structure immediately begins to cloud.

No duties for the position of executive liaison are outlined in the A-MEG charter, so it becomes necessary to rely on interviews and observations to determine the function of this office. The commander of A-MEG states that the executive liaison is strictly a communication link between A-MEG and the board. The executive liaison reports that he is a "liaison" between the board and the commander, and that he "oversees activities" and "advises" the board.

He further states that he acts as the command authority over the A-MEG commander. A high-ranking County Sheriff Department official who helped bring about the A-MEG unit sees the executive liaison as having a "dual role" both as a communicative link between the unit and the board and as an administrator over the unit commander regarding C-City concerns (whatever these might be). These are markedly different views.

It rapidly becomes apparent that the role of the executive liaison is a source of great confusion to those who have sought to implement the A-MEG plan. By placing the executive liaison operationally superior to the commander in the mind of the former, but not the latter, the chain of command is muddled and lines of authority have become confused. By conferring operational authority on the commander and, to a great extent, administrative authority also the planners have split the executive role between him and the executive liaison.

Many problems of implementation and operation have resulted from the fragmentation of administrative authority as well as from similar flaws in other areas, such as recordkeeping and job specialization. A-MEG has been plagued by breakdowns in communication and by such aberrations as overspecialization and renewed jurisdictional fragmentation. Time and again the unit has failed to achieve a tightly coordinated and well-directed effort. Examples of failed implementation abound.

A prime example is the breakdown of *centralized operational command*.[5] Without question, those personnel who have been deputized by the sheriff and who have been assigned to A-MEG are under one unified command. All case assignments are made by the commander, and special titles and areas of responsibility held by the investigators are determined by him. He reports to the executive liaison and the board on the activities and accomplishments of A-MEG, and receives mission responsibilities from them. However, a rival unit came onto the scene subsequent to the formation of A-MEG. C-City continued to experience the difficult problem of drug warfare and drug houses. Pressure to do something about it continued to increase on political leaders in the city council and in the office of the mayor. At the same time the A-MEG commander saw his mission as the interdiction of high-level drug trafficking and the targeting of drug kingpins; he resisted the reassignment of A-MEG investigators to the street-level problem. As a result, an existing vice unit of the CCPD became charged with neutralizing the street dealers and drug houses. Its staff was doubled and its budget was increased. Before long, the vice unit commander began to expand the scope of his unit's role to large-scale conspiracy investigations, and he began to ask for assistance from A-MEG for his own caseload. Soon CCPD vice and A-MEG began tripping over each other in the field, and, once again the two largest jurisdictions of the county were in competition and at cross-purposes.

Another salient instance of implementation failure is in the area of specialization. Unfortunately, A-MEG experienced a great deal of difficulty as a result of what appears to be an attempt to overspecialize. For one thing, there were far more specialties and titles than investigators. In one instance a single investigator found himself being a case manager, computer intelligence analyst, marijuana eradication officer, and photographer. Of course, it was not long until problems of coordination and complaints by personnel that they were overtaxed occurred. Efforts to cope with these problems resulted in even more complications. For example, a new form was generated to facilitate requests for particular actions by the various specialists. The Field Action Request was a form that any given case manager (the lead agent on a case) would fill out to request action such as video surveillance of a location or person. These forms were to be routed to the commander, who would assign the action to the pertinent specialist. The particular specialist would perform the action and route the results back to the commander for review. The commander would then route the results back to the requesting case manager. These forms were in use for only a matter of weeks, then simply fell into disuse. This difficulty continued, as did similar problems after equally ineffective solutions were tried.

A-MEG has never overcome this inability to coordinate activity. Many times it has sought to bring about a more integrated effort by its personnel, but without success. Minutes of staff meetings abound with reorganizations having such titles as Reestablishment of Team Effort in [A-MEG] Operations and Four Philosophies of [A-MEG]. The history of A-MEG specialization has been one of constant breakdown and resultant factionalism, and reorganization efforts have continued to the present day. Somehow the unit has never come to grips with the fact that it has overspecialized.

In virtually every area of implementation A-MEG would receive a negative evaluation, be it in one of those areas already examined or in centralized communications and centralized budgeting. Yet the program continued to be funded and supported by those in power. Indeed, it was lauded by them. Why was this so?

TWO POSSIBLE REALITIES

Two plausible explanations might account for why A-MEG, despite its failures, continued to be touted as a viable program for fighting the war on drugs. The first would contend that there was simply a lack of understanding. Under this scheme one would see A-MEG as an organization in search of an identity, the victim of incrementalism gone amok. The failure to effectively centralize command could be attributed to an inability of those charged with instituting the unit to comprehend the flaw inherent in confusing the roles of commander and executive liaison. The quagmire of overspecialization could be blamed on the uncertain nature of the tasks presented to the unit and the generally heuristic environment into which the investigators and their

commander were thrust.   In other words, this view would find that the
participants in the A-MEG experiment were in over their heads.

A competing explanation exists as well.   There are those who have written
extensively on the importance of hidden agendas and of political scams in the
field of criminal justice.   Such writers as Jeffrey Reiman, Rick Lovell, and Stan
Stojkovic would contend that one might be able to explain the failure to
implement a sound design for A-MEG by regarding it as an acceptable result
on the part of the politicians and officials charged with that responsibility.   In
his book *The Rich Get Richer and the Poor Get Prison*, Reiman writes: "I
propose that we can make more sense out of criminal justice policy by
assuming that its goal is to maintain crime than by assuming that its goal is to
reduce crime!"[6]   Reiman believes that this is so in a de facto sense: that the
class nature of street crime is conducive to such an effect.   The poor, he asserts,
are those most affected by such crime and are also those least capable of
influencing criminal justice policy so as to counter it.   At the same time, the
wealthy gain from identifying crime with the poorer classes and with the failure
of the criminal justice system to cope with crime, and thus have no incentive to
improve such policies themselves.   Those in the best position to effect positive
change, therefore, do not.   The effect is thus an acceptable result rather than a
conspiratorial intent, but the effect is still real.   The status quo continues.

Lovell and Stojkovic have written on how myths and symbols are generated
by correctional administrators in response to the power structures that control
prison resources so as to mask the true nature of policy-making in their
institutions and to preserve the status quo.[7]   The myth that prisons are engaged
in the business of rehabilitation is perpetuated by corrections officials to placate
a legislature and public that buy into the rehabilitative ideal.   Meanwhile, the
two assert, what prisons actually do is warehouse people.   Another such myth
discussed by Lovell and Stojkovic is that societal protection is achieved by
prisons via the mechanism of incapacitation.   They demonstrate that this is not
supported statistically: "Although some argue that incapacitation reduces the
rate of serious crime (see Blumstein et al, 1978), data from the National Crime
Survey indicate that rates of violent crime remain quite high, fluctuating during
the past fifteen years over a range of from 32 to 38 violent victimizations per
1,000 residents age 12 and older"[8]

Lovell and Stojkovic go on to contend that such a myth serves to mask the
fact that the goal of expanding the number of prison beds and, therefore, the job
security of correctional officials is the true policy of such administrators.   They
contend that myths such as these and the symbolic responses of correctional
officials (e.g., the inclusion of general education degree programs in prisons)
serve to deflect public attention from the actual policy-making processes, which
are designed to support the political and economic interests of those in power.
Such myths and the symbolic responses of prison administrators to them serve

merely to protect the status quo–to shield the true policy-making process from the influence of external forces.

No doubt some would contend that the generation of myths by the power structure of the County and the provision of symbolic responses to them by A-MEG is what has been occurring in the program under examination. After all, law enforcement was no longer able to contend that it was successfully engaging and controlling the criminal element in the County–or across the country. In the grant application, the implementers of A-MEG readily admitted that local law enforcement had failed to deal with the drug crisis. In the creation of a national drug tsar, the federal government had also conceded an inability to cope with the "drug war." Hence the need to generate a new myth. Law enforcement was in "need" of a new concept to compete with the better-equipped drug lords of the modern era. A new synergism "had" to be found if victory was to be achieved. The answer was to be the metropolitan enforcement group. Law enforcement clamored for it. The federal government provided for it. The program became a reality.

There is at least tacit evidence to support such a contention regarding the A-MEG program. It is hard to believe that the implementers of A-MEG could not be aware of the failings within the unit that have become apparent. Surely they must have been aware that its unwieldy structure would be a difficult administrative problem at best. It also seems unlikely that the board could avoid detecting the many debacles that were occurring. Nor does it seem reasonable that the executive liaison would find the development of a rival narcotics unit conducive to the consolidation of drug enforcement resources. Such a halfhearted level of commitment by the implementers of the A-MEG program supports the contention that it is actually a symbolic response to the political and public pressures of the time.

It is interesting to note that centralization was most salient in the area of equipment. If there is one thing impressive about the A-MEG unit, it is its hardware. The unit has a room filled with state-of-the-art surveillance equipment. It also possesses three PC computer systems. Such impressive contraptions tend to serve as symbols in the "war on drugs." So do newspaper headlines concerning the new metropolitan enforcement groups and the sophistication they are supposed to bring to bear on the drug crisis. It is telling.

A SYNTHESIS

Each of the explanations offered above has merit. It is difficult to conceive of the organizers of A-MEG as anything other than bureaucrats. They were police chiefs and other administrators faced with the need for budget. At the same time it is equally difficult to conclude that none of them desired to implement an effective program to combat drug crimes. Persons of differing motives and individuals with multiple intentions must have been actors within this framework. Some had budget as a primary goal. Others were looking for a more effective enforcement unit. Some needed personnel that they otherwise could not obtain for their agencies. Doubtless there were those who hoped to achieve all these benefits. Police administrators do not set out to avoid enforcing the drug laws any more than correctional officials set out to ensure a ready stock of recidivists. They do, however, set out to maximize budget and expand their area of influence. It is a primary goal of any bureaucracy to survive and grow.

That the need to survive became the dominant theme at A-MEG is arguable, for it cannot be believed that the chief executives of the coalition departments were unaware of the unit's developing problems. Political necessity must have been the driving force that caused them to remain steadfast behind A-MEG. The need for resources caused them to turn a blind eye. If effectiveness were the overriding concern of the board, it would have pursued some other practical course of action that was more consistent with a dedicated intent once the program had floundered. They did not.

THE MORAL

It is obvious by now that issues of ethics and morality have entered into the implementation process. Failed ethics can account for the promulgation of a fraud–that A-MEG was the best solution to the drug problem. Those who continued to support what they knew to be a failed program out of political "necessity" sold out. Those who knew from the start that such a convoluted structure was doomed to failure betrayed the public trust. Those who had genuine hopes that A-MEG could be effective are the only participants who can be exonerated, for though they were mistaken, they fought the good fight.

Thus, both of two plausible realities are represented here. There exists a champion for the stated agenda of battling drugs and one for the hidden goals of organizational survival and political advantage.

In sum–and to be coldly objective–some did indeed buy into the stated goals of A-MEG. But ostensible goals are just that–ostensible. It just might be that the hidden agenda referred to above has truly eclipsed those goals. If this is assumed to be true, then what little success has been achieved by A-MEG has been accomplished in spite of the actual intentions of the bulk of the actors within the organization. An even more cynical view would be that these accomplishments came about only because they comprised just enough success to gain the political advantage necessary to insure the positions of administrators and politicians.

Perhaps professional leadership is analogous to military leadership. One must daily wade into the fray as a knight into battle, sword drawn and battle plan at the ready. For there are countless villains on the field of battle; and others, misguided, will hinder virtue. One must ever keep sight of one's banner and of the objective ahead. A leader must never become distracted from virtue and cause. To lead, one must confront the enemy, for there is no justice without a champion and there will be no champion to come forward unless it is you.

NOTES

1. Rickey D. Lashley, "Limited Centralization of a Metropolitan Enforcement Group: A Case Study" (Master's Paper, University of Wisconsin-Milwuakee, 1991).

2. Walter F. Baber, *Organizing the Future* (Birmingham, AL, 1983), 38.

3. Ibid., 31.

4. Lashley, 22-24.

5. Ibid., 26-27.

6. Jeffrey H. Reiman, *The Rich Get Richer and the Poor Get Prison* (New York, 1979), 16.

7. Rick Lovell and Stan Stojkovic, "Myths, Symbols, and Policymaking in Corrections," in *Criminal Justice Policy Review*, ed. Robert Mutchnick (Indiana, PA, 1987), vol.2, no.3.

8. Ibid., 229.

Part II

THE WAR ON DRUGS, THE WAR ON CRIME, AND BATTLES THAT WERE NEVER FOUGHT

5

The Armistice

Among the worst consequences resulting from a lack of fidelity to justice in the field of policework is the existence of a tacit understanding between law enforcement and certain criminal elements. There are, unfortunately, lines of demarcation between criminals and police–protocols, as it were. They are evidenced by such expressions as "Keep it off the street" and "You're just doing your job." Police officers are known to state the former as a requirement to certain violators, and offenders have been known to indicate understanding by stating the latter to the police.

Many an officer will tell you that there are certain neighborhoods over which they have little or no control. Some of the more candid will, as well, point out that certain classes of criminals are seemingly immune to police authority. It is the rare officer who will claim to have the upper hand in an inner city housing project, and the well-heeled crime boss is hardly ever brought to justice. At the same time a certain minimal level of order and safety is maintained for mainstream America, as is evidenced by the fact that most citizens are able to make their way to work and engage in recreation during their leisure time. Factories produce, universities educate and explore, and tourists see the sights of the many cities and towns that make up our country. These are the demilitarized zones of America.

We tolerate a certain level of crime so long as it does not, by and large, disrupt the ability of the society to function. This occurs for quite practical reasons. It allows the operation of the underground economy that serves to supplement the legitimate system of wealth distribution. It manages crime so that it does not spill over into the business districts and the "good part of town." In short, it is functional-some would even say healthy.

Prostitution is never eradicated. It is only contained. Drug abuse was not recognized as a literal crisis until it began to debilitate the mainstream economy and to infiltrate middle America. Organized crime continues to thrive, so long as it adheres to certain conventions, such as discreet behavior and limiting itself to areas of crime such as gambling and insurance fraud.

Attacking such problems and criminal organizations is difficult and dangerous–genuinely dangerous. It is not easy to ferret out prostitution and drug trafficking operations. The cases are hard to build and to prosecute. It is a deadly business to penetrate a criminal ring, and such work takes both an emotional and a physical toll on the law enforcement officer who attempts it. I served in the field of policework for fourteen years, nearly six of those in drug enforcement. Not only is it possible for me to cite statistics to corroborate these assertions[1] but I can testify directly to the paniclike fear that all but overwhelms an officer operating undercover and in the midst of an illicit drug deal.

There are tough decisions that must be made and dangerous risks that must be taken in order to impact on the violence and corruption that assault our society. Inevitably, officers will die. Invariably, administrators must choose whether to strike a deal with the devil or die a professional death in the community in where they work. Lines have been drawn. Compromises have been made. And, of course, rationalizations have been put into place to allow for denial, both psychological and political.

Evidence of such a line of demarcation comes from a contrast between the modern era and certain earlier periods in the history of law enforcement. The time of prohibition provides one such contrast. The rise of organized crime and the attempt to control its bootleging operations took a terrible toll in lives and violence in the street. Yet, tacitly, politicians and officials tolerated bootlegging–even patronized the speakeasies that sold illicit alcohol. And when the violence rose to war zone proportions and the price of victory over organized crime was recognized as enormous sacrifice and expense, the government simply gave up. Prohibition was repealed.

The modern era has been one of peaceful coexistence and of relative calm. Until recently, machine gun battles were uncommon on the streets of America and the truce served quite well. But an unfortunate parallel to the time of prohibition is occurring in the 1990s. As was hinted above, the reality of drug addiction and its impact on the middle class represent a breach of the protocols. Of course, the parties to the compact have changed. The drug cartels have invaded, and so have the wantonly violent gangs that control the American market. The Jamaican Posse, the Colombian drug lords and the "gang bangers" are of a different breed than were the more civilized gangsters who preceded them.

Machine gun battles have returned to our streets. The murder rates in our cities are at all time highs. Indeed, foreign governments have begun to provide travel advisories warning their citizens of violence in our tourist centers. Our schools turn up handguns in locker inspections, and some have even found it necessary to limit outdoor recess due to gunfire and homicides in the neighborhood.

Yet even in the alarm of this moment, the police still adhere to the terms of a truce that has been hopelessly shattered. To be sure, peace officers carry bigger and more destructive firearms, Uzis and semiautomatic pistols abound, and many raids are conducted on the drug houses and street corner operations of the local drug distributors. But, while the police lock up violators by the thousands, the reality that little is being accomplished begins to surface in the courts.

The federal government has encouraged local law enforcement to team up with the U.S. attorneys in prosecuting dangerous drug felons.[2] Federal authorities believed that the mandatory and lengthy sentences available in the federal courts would be more effective than local laws in combating the distribution of illicit drugs. What has happened instead is a flooding of the federal court system with petty criminals. Predictably, the federal judiciary has begun to call a halt to it all.[3] Judges complain bitterly that their courts are overloaded to the point that they cannot function effectively and that more important cases are shunted aside by petty ones. Restrictions have come down to the effect that asset seizures are now rejected if they do not represent extremely large amounts of cash or valuables. Agents and police officers are chided for charging petty criminals under the federal statutes. U.S. attorneys are exasperated in their efforts to get local law enforcement agencies to concentrate on large-scale conspiracies and big money criminal enterprises. This is even the case with federally funded drug task forces.

Recently, an assistant U.S. attorney, lecturing before a group of drug enforcement officers, implored the investigators to pursue the sophisticated rings that continue to escape their efforts. I spoke with him afterward and we discussed how difficult it is to focus the attention of police administrators on such organizations. He seemed at a loss, and at the end of our conversation, I was not quite certain whether he attributed the problem to the penchant of police officials to chase statistics or to their lack of understanding as to the most efficacious policy of enforcement.

The response of the police to the drug war is perhaps more complicated than was revealed in my conversation with the able attorney. Police administrators do chase statistics. After all, they are bureaucrats. There may also be a lack of understanding because law enforcement has never completely professionalized its management. There are police executives heading departments with hundreds of officers on staff who do not even hold a bachelor's degree in any field, let alone police science or public administration. There is also the reality of politics and corruption. And then there is the safety of avoiding a direct confrontation with organized crime. In light of all of this, it should be no wonder that rounding up street-level marijuana and cocaine dealers takes up most of the time the police devote to drug enforcement.

The armistice, I believe, is the most explanatory of all the possibilities. How else could one account for the relative indifference of the police to the problem of organized crime? The streets of America are no longer safe. Gangs and disorder are rampant. People are dying by the hundreds at the hands of the "gang bangers" and the fuel for the violence is supplied by organized crime in the form of cocaine.

Interestingly, the call for repeal of prohibition is rising to the fore once again. As the case for abandoning the prohibition of alcohol was made in the 1920s so the rhetoric has begun that calls for repeal of the laws against the possession and use of narcotics and other dangerous drugs. Intellectuals such as William F. Buckley, Jr., and Milton Friedman as well as such public leaders as former Secretary of State George P. Shultz and New York City Police Commissioner Patrick V. Murphy have begun the call to repeal such statutes.[4] They would simply give up, thinking it hopeless to resist the flow of drugs.

There will be no retreat this time, however. Cocaine and its counterparts present a different level of threat than were the distilleries of the 1920s. It is an enemy that gives no quarter, and it knows no code of conduct or civilized rules of engagement. It will ravage us if it goes unchallenged, and no one comprehends this better than the police. In my travels as a narcotics investigator, I have seen no more powerful agent of destruction than cocaine. I have witnessed the prostitution of an addict's own wife-by the addict himself-in exchange for a little bag of white powder for his pipe. I have known people to steal from their own family and betray their closest friends in order to satisfy their lust for their drug. It destroys the will, and so it can destroy a nation. One need only look to the recent past-for instance, to the Opium Wars between China and Great Britain-to realize that this is so.

There is no logic to the legalization of dangerous drugs. Such an approach is more than a surrender. It borders on complicity. There can be no retreat in the present situation. And, as the enemy has already demonstrated, it knows no compassion for its captives. There can be no hope for quarter today. There will be no armistice this time. As evidence of this, the reader is offered an example of the kind of battles that lie ahead in Chapter 6.

NOTES

1. Robert M. Stutman and Richard Esposito, *Dead on Delivery* (New York, 1992), 44-45.

2. Rickey D. Lashley, "Limited Centralization of a Metropolitan Enforcement Group: A Case Study" (Master's Paper, University of Wisconsin-Milwaukee, 1991), 1-4.

3. "Some Call for a Drug Cease-fire," Racine Journal Times, July 11, 1992, la.

4. Ibid.

6

Joe

The agent felt uneasy staring through the windshield of his car, all too aware that he was likely to be discovered sitting alone this late at night. He settled low into the seat, peering over the dash in crab fashion, hopeful that soon he would be joined by another member of his unit. It was getting cold, but the officer knew how foolish it would be to start the engine with its telltale exhaust and, so he pulled up the collar of his raid jacket. He was glad to have played it cautious. The target was pulling to the curb in front of the house he had been watching since 11:05 that evening. It was 12:15 A.M. now, and the officer pulled the radio mike close to his lips to notify the base, "He's in the pocket."

Aware that other units were scrambling to arrive before the target could leave the house, the agent felt his pulse begin to quicken. SWAT, too, was racing to assemble and make the scene. It would be a dangerous raid tonight. A veteran of the so-called drug war, the investigator had been through the door on many an occasion prior to this one, but never had the prospects been so ominous. The target, Joe, was known to him. The officer had been his jailer back in the 1980s when the inmate had paid another detainee a carton of commissary cigarettes to jump off a cell bunk and brake Joe's leg in an effort to force a trip outside the jail. Joe was a wild one indeed, and tonight officers had intelligence that he was in possession of a bomb.

The agent's thoughts were interrupted by the arrival of a second undercover unit. The agent's partner said that he was in position to the north. A few minutes later the two were advised by the supervisor that the raid team was on the way.

There was no need to ask for further instructions. The briefing had already taken place. A signal would be given for the SWAT team to make entry. Metro units would hold position until the SWAT unit had begun its assault on the building entrances and then move in to maintain a perimeter outside the house. If things went as usual, the residence would be secured in less than ten seconds, its occupants in handcuffs and all rooms cleared.

The next few minutes passed without incident, and the remaining narcotics squads took up positions to the south, east, and west. The agent and his partner kept their eyes on the target's residence lest some movement go undetected and the advantage be lost. Incredulous, they observed the SWAT team swarming onto the curtilage of the target house. There had been a mix-up in the signal. Realizing that the other metro units on the outer perimeter might not be aware that the raid had begun, one of them said into the radio, "SWAT is on the move." Left with the option of doing nothing or moving in, the narcotics units ran in behind SWAT.

The agents could already hear the crash of the battering ram against the front door of the house as they ran onto the lawn and toward their appointed posts on the perimeter. The first, known as the Professor, was to take the northeast corner of the home while his partner, Beetle, made for the west side of the house along the north wall. It was then that the two of them realized just how desperately wrong the plan had gone. The crashing had stopped and the scream "Police, search warrant." was no longer heard. The entire operation seemed to catch its breath for an instant. The agents witnessed something to they had never experienced before-the SWAT team was retreating. At the same time they could hear the controlled voice of a SWAT officer's voice: "He has the device."

The agents swallowed hard. A second SWAT member notified his commander, in that matter-of-fact way that only the tactical officers have, "I can take him. He's in my sights." At the same time they heard the target's frantic voice, "Get back. I'll do it. I swear I'll do it." The narcotics agents realized that the suspect had produced the bomb they had been warned about and he was threatening to use it.

The suspect had met the SWAT entry team inside the home, accompanied by his girlfriend and holding an explosive device. Upon seeing the bomb, the team had grabbed the woman and retreated through the door they had entered. The suspect had followed them to the door and was threatening to blow up the officers if they did not leave. Most of the SWAT team took up defensive positions behind the automobiles lining the street in front of the residence. One of them found himself against the north wall of the house together with Beetle and the Professor. There the three of them, along with Ken, another metro agent who had been attempting to take a position on the perimeter, found themselves trapped. They would not be able to proceed west along the wall because they would have to climb a fence between the target house and the one next to it. The obstacle was not so high that this could not be done physically, but if they did so, the officers would be visible through two large windows. The suspect could be heard only a few feet away, shouting threats at the police outside. They would have to stay where they were and rely on the ingenuity and training of SWAT to get them out.

The tactical team set up a command post from which to negotiate with Joe, the target of the raid. They went about the business of evacuating the neighbors and establishing an open phone line with the crazed suspect who was holding them all hostage as they raced to stabilize the scene. As they worked, Joe continued to scream that he would "take one of you with me." He also demanded that the police leave the area-an action that simply would not occur.

So began the standoff. Although the trapped officers would eventually be evacuated to a safe perimeter, not all would end so well. Throughout the night they waited and, as these things tend to do, the site of the standoff soon became a media circus. By daybreak the TV crews were on the scene; a camera to the north, another two to the south. Reporters were everywhere. Crowds had built up, and patrol had its hands full holding back gawkers. Children had to be routed around the site of the standoff as they made their way to school. All the while the police negotiator was on the phone, either talking to Joe trying to get him to pick up the receiver and talk to him again.

Joe was erratic, one minute telling the negotiator how he wished to put this behind him and the next minute insisting that he would not be taken alive. As night turned to day, the police began to realize more and more what the likely result would be. The officers were exhausted now. Thanks to the Fire Bells, a volunteer auxiliary of the Fire Department, they had fought off the cold with coffee and pastry while taking turns warming themselves in their converted rescue truck. But coffee would not keep them going for a second night, and they knew it. They were losing their edge, and it was difficult to concentrate. It was time to make a decision.

Down came the drill from the command on scene. They would end it today, before school was dismissed at two o'clock. The teams that were now in place would stay in place, and they would either assault the house or force Joe from it. Supervisors were called to the command post to receive detailed orders for their subordinates.

Then the first of the concussion grenades went off inside the house, quickly followed by the sound of breaking glass as the windows were blown out. The grenadiers launched tear gas through the newly broken window panes. The gawkers gasped, and some of them even screamed. Then silence.

Almost beyond the agents' belief, Joe could be seen through the now glassless windows, still defiant and refusing to come out. The SWAT team continued to order him to put down his device and exit through the doorway, but he refused.

A second round of concussion grenades and tear gas was ordered, and once again the SWAT team delivered their payloads into the house. Still defiant, but unable to endure the barrage any longer, Joe stepped onto the stoop outside the side doorway. The explosive device was still visible in his hands, one hand holding the explosive and the other the detonator. SWAT ordered him to put down the device or be shot, and he took a step forward. Over the radio could be heard the voice of a SWAT team commander as he gave the order, "He is not to step off the porch with that device." Joe moved, and stepped off the landing and onto the steps. The commander ordered his sniper to fire if Joe made a move off the steps and onto the yard.

And then it happened. Joe took the last step he would ever take and as he did so, he pulled the fuse and hurled the device at the front line of the SWAT team perimeter. There was a furious explosion as the bomb detonated in front of the team. No sooner had it done so than they could hear the deadly reports of the sniper's rifle as he fired two well-placed rounds into the suspect's chest. And in a chilling staccato lasting well beyond the crack of the rifle, a machine gun burst raked across the suspect's body.

It is a serious conflict, this war on drugs, and, sadly, it parallels in so many respects another of our country's most tragic battles. We limit our efforts to firefights in the back country and our targets to those of minor strategic importance. The Caribbean and Latin America have become our present-day Ho Chi Minh Trail. Bolivia and Colombia are our Cambodia and North Vietnam.

But the war we fight in the 1990s is far more dangerous than the one from which we extricated ourselves in 1975, for today we are fighting for our very existence as a nation. There is no retreat from a foreign theater of battle available to us now. The enemy is upon us. Our borders have been breached. We are overrun.

And yet we fight this conflict as impotently as we fought in Vietnam. The scenario is the same. Our politicians have tried to run the war as though a major conflagration were a minor police action. Vietnam was not Grenada, and America's fight with the cartels is not the effort to enforce alternate side of the street parking. Drug cartels with assets larger than many a national budget are combining with each other to assault our borders and ravage our population. It is an enormous alliance that we face, and yet we hail poster campaigns and police task forces that are undermanned and poorly directed as our solutions rather than take the fight to the cartels.

In no way do I demean the integrity of the officers with whom I served in this effort. Many have devoted their careers to protecting the public. Some have lost their lives. But we will never defeat an enemy we are unwilling to fully engage. The police are not an army. They could never pretend to defeat one in battle. Yet they are all we have sent out to face the legions of the drug lords.

There will be other raids that end like the one described above in many other towns across this country, and as in Southeast Asia, the victims of these skirmishes will always be innocent citizens caught in the cross fire as well as the veterans of the conflict, our police.

Let there be no doubt as to the message I intend: that these are only holding actions in a war that will seem to have no end until we as a people and our leaders in government decide enough is enough and take the battle to the enemy. Police officers should keep the peace of the community, not fight the wars of the nation.

I was present the day we took Joe's life, and I will never forget the face of that sniper after he climbed down from the roof of the building across the street from Joe's house. Neither will I ever forget the sound of my good friend crying in despair because he could not talk the suspect into surrender. Such sights and sounds will always be with us, to be sure, but we should minimize the need to endure them.

7

The Forgotten Wars

The "forgotten wars" are, oddly enough, precisely those that are most glorified by the mythology of our time. The cocaine cartels of South America comprise the greatest menace to grace the front covers of our national magazines in decades, and they loom large beneath the banner headlines of the country's newspapers. *U.S. News & World Report*, for example, devoted nine pages of its August 19, 1991, issue to the crack problem alone. On the front page of the January 26, 1990, issue of *USA Today* the headline at the top of the page reads "Bush: 'Whatever it takes' on drugs." Scattered about me on the floor of my library as I write these lines is a collection of publications filled with hundreds of pages of strategies, statistics, summaries and proclamations which have emanated from the White House between 1988 and 1992. They are known collectively as the National Drug Control Strategies and are commonly referred to as the Red Book, Green Book, or White Book, according to the year of issue. Inside of each, is a facsimile of a letter to the Congress of the United States, bearing the signature of President George Bush. In the September 1989 issue the president speaks forcefully of America's commitment to the war on drugs:

This report is the product of an unprecedented national effort over many months. America's fight against epidemic illegal drug use cannot be won on any single front alone; it must be waged everywhere—at every level of Federal, State, and local government and by every citizen in every community across the country.[1]

And the White House is not alone in its zeal to champion the eradication of drugs in America. Lying among the scattered strategy books of the Bush administration are such reports and programs as *The Attorney General's Strategy: Combating Narcotics in the Nineties,*[2] *Drug Enforcement and Prosecution in the '90's,*[3] and *Communities Take Action: A Governor's Conference on Juvenile Crime, Drugs, and Gangs.*[4] The first of these is a publication issued by Donald J. Hanaway while he was the attorney general for the state of Wisconsin. This report cites the drug problem as being a grave one and confesses, "We are losing the war on drugs"[5] The latter two are efforts by state-level agencies which are tasked with assisting in the fight against drugs inside the borders of the state of Wisconsin.

Public perception regarding the confrontation between the legitimate agencies of government and the illicit organizations of the criminal elements of our society and the larger world is that we are locked in a battle for our very existence as a nation. The conflict has been portrayed as tantamount to the great wars of our century. The rhetoric of the drug war conjures up images of the battlefronts of World War II and of the victory gardens and rubber drives on the home front in 1940s America. Yet, while it is all too evident that the present threat to our security as a nation and to the peace of our neighborhoods is just as real as was that of the Axis, our response to it has been merely to rattle sabers and instigate meaningless skirmishes.

Bravado has never won a war. Rhetoric and marketing will never convince an aggressor to retreat. Slogans and committees will not suffice where blood and steel are the measure of a victory. The "gang bangers" and the cartels are not persuaded by a policy statement. Organized crime is never defeated by proclamation. Politicians and bureaucrats who engage in such symbolic gestures are merely whistling in the graveyard. The sound of their own voices comforts them and allows them to feel they have accomplished some good. Pathetically, they will assert that they are championing the cause.

Among the many documents I have mentioned in these last few paragraphs lies yet another report from yet another commission that addresses the problem of drugs in America. Much to my chagrin, the first signature at the bottom of the preface is my own. The Conference Series Report is yet another example of how misplaced priorities can blunt the good intentions of some and serve the need for political window dressing of others. Just as A-MEG facilitated the myriad interests of politicians and bureaucrats while doing little or nothing for the stated mission of the drug agents who comprised it, so the commission succeeded in deflecting criticism from politicians but precious little else.

In the summer of 1989 the various law enforcement agencies in my community found themselves in the midst of a turf battle. There were numerous homicides; victims were being found murdered execution style and gunned down as the result of drive-by shootings. The limited resources of the police department and its elite Street Crimes Unit, as well as the county's Metro Drug Unit, on which I served at the time, were strained beyond their capacity. The gangs were challenging the police for control of the streets.

It was not long before church groups and community organizations began to clamor for action. Both the mayor and the county executive came under public pressure to do something about the problem. There were marches and rallies and a great deal of press. Politicians responded.

What the politicians did, however, was not to double the size of the Metro Drug Unit, nor did they divert large numbers of officers to neighborhood patrols. Certainly there was no escalation of the effort to interdict drug shipments on the interstate highway or at the rail and bus terminals. There was no substantive change in the commitment of resources that local government devoted to drug enforcement. What did occur was that local politicians called for a new commission to study the problem and recommend corrective action.

The commission was brought into existence with great fanfare; scores of citizens were appointed to a variety of committees charged with exploring particular areas such as legislation or youth efforts, and then reporting back to the mayor and the county executive. A great deal of effort was expended by a large number of volunteers. Thousands of dollars of tax money was spent as well. The result of all this was a youth conference held at the local university, a conference series on juvenile crime and drug abuse, and a handful of similar events affecting the policies of local and state government only slightly.

I was a graduate student during the time this commission was in place, attending classes one or two nights a week when not serving search warrants and arresting drug pushers. The subject of one of my papers was the drug problem and efforts to deal with it. While researching it, I came into contact with the drug commission and was invited to join it.

Eventually, I served as the chairman of the Criminal Justice Committee and had occasion to speak with one of the administrators of the state Office of Justice Administration (OJA). He told me that his agency had failed to use all of its allocated grant monies for the 1991 budget year, so I offered to write a grant application for a large share of the overage my-committee had not been provided with a budget.[6] He was happy to entertain such a request but told me that I had only about sixty days in which to spend the money because of the administrative requirement that it be expended by that date or returned to the federal government.

Thence began a feverish effort to use a windfall and somehow make progress with the mandate to investigate the problems of drug abuse and violent crime. I hurriedly drafted the application for the grant and, by using the fax machine, managed to reduce the approval process to only a few days. Hasty committee meetings were held and an agenda was put together. Before the grant window had closed, we had managed to spend all the money allotted to the commission by OJA.

We held a conference and a few follow up meetings, but the agenda that was established for the conference was not exactly what we would have liked to sponsor. The grant money that was available to us was earmarked by the federal government for juvenile matters and could not be applied to another purpose. This forced us to tailor the conference to juvenile issues.

The conference was therefore a meeting on juvenile crime and drug abuse. This would not cover our larger mandate, but it was the only way we could afford to assemble a representative body of officials and experts from around the state on any aspect of the drug problem, so we proceeded. There were also a few follow-up meetings of a small group of the original attendees to pursue the recommendations that came out of the initial conference. The final result was the short, five page report to which I have earlier referred.

The commission was disbanded early in 1992, long after the heated turf war of the summer of 1989. Few of its recommendations had any substantive impact on county or city government. Certainly the commission had little to do with how local officials coped with the spate of homicides.

What officials did do that summer was crack down hard on selected groups of cocaine dealers and their enforcers. At the Metro Drug Unit we were charged with taking out a given set of targets marked for arrest. We set about the business of doing so, using undercover buy operations, heavy surveillance, and infiltration by informants. The Street Crimes Unit had its own short list as well. Many of the operations were successful, and the number of murders did go down-for a while.

Yet the problem of drugs and drug-related crime has not truly abated here, just as it has continued to plague the rest of America. In 1994, the community's serious crime rate is still high. By 1992 it had become the highest in the state. Killings that would have made the front page of the newspaper for days on end in decades past, today warrant only brief mention in the local press.

It is telling that the forgotten wars are those about which stories are most often told. Tragically, we shine only in moments of desperation, and our finest hours are fleeting. The concentrated efforts of the agencies responsible for drug enforcement in my home county should not represent only the stopgap measure they unfortunately became that summer. Rather, fewer police officers should be serving as parking meter checkers, revenue generators, and public relations officers, and more of them should be assigned to disrupting drug distribution networks. There should be a good deal less emphasis on generating calls for service reports and a great deal more on penetrating organized crime rings. Certainly there needs to be far less time spent on following patrol officers to see whether they take a twenty-five-minute lunch break instead of a twenty-minute one, and far more ferreting out the intelligence leaks that plague investigations of organized cocaine rings.

From suburban Wisconsin to the borders of the nation, the forgotten wars exist beneath the noses of our government. From city hall to the halls of Congress the battles which must be fought if we are to emerge victorious are ignored in preference for window dressing. There is talk of supply-side enforcement and border interdiction. Some officials call for cooperative efforts with drug-producing countries via economic subsidies. Washington rails against the cartels, yet spends most of its allocations on feel-good programs. Foundations and committees abound whose primary purpose seems to be the administration of 800 number hot lines through which one can order brochures. Everywhere there have sprung up organizations, apparently designed to expend grant money-for they seem to do little else. They generate slogans and issue policy recommendations but do little to eradicate addiction and crime.

The federal government has been budgeting an additional $10 to $12 billion annually these past few years in the effort to win the war on drugs. This would hardly seem to match the magnitude of a wartime effort, considering that it took some $40 billion to prosecute the Persian Gulf conflict. Certainly we are not in any danger of suffering a Pyrrhic victory over the drug lords of Colombia and Peru. It would take an effort many times larger than what is currently being brought to bear in order to overcome the vast resources of the cartels and of the organized crime rings, within our own borders.

So what must we do to achieve victory in the war to eradicate drugs in America? We must do the obvious. Officers must be diverted from pushing paper and collecting revenue and reassigned to narcotics units and criminal intelligence. Drug task forces must be given teeth and provided not only with sophisticated equipment and weapons but also with independence of operation and centralized authority, to enable them to act decisively. It may even be necessary to delegate such responsibilities to special state police units with a level of manpower and expertise not currently found in the police services. And there is more.

The local police cannot be expected to deal with problems that are more properly the responsibility of the federal government. Drug trafficking is an international problem with international implications. The marijuana fields and the coca plantations of Mexico and South America can never be affected by the detectives of small town America. If Washington is truly committed to stopping the flow of drugs, it will have to pursue a foreign policy that is designed to do so. Economic subsidies and diplomatic pressure will never be a substitute for hard action. In any event, until the government of the United States comes to grips with protecting its own borders, the police departments of the fifty states can hardly be expected to eradicate the illicit drug trade within them. So long as we all keep our heads in the sand, the problem will continue to overwhelm us.

NOTES

1. *National Drug Control Strategy* (Washington D.C.: The White House, 1989), p. ii.

2. Donald J. Hanaway, *The Attorney General's Strategy: Combating Narcotics in the Nineties* (Madison: Office of the Attorney General of the State of Wisconsin, 1989).

3. *Drug Enforcement Prosecution in the '90's: A Conference Report* (Madison: Wisconsin Office of Justice Assistance, 1992).

4.   *Communities Take Action: A Conference Report* (Milwaukee, WI: Wisconsin Office of Justice Assistance, 1992).

5.   Hanaway, p. 4.

6.   It is very telling that an executive of government would establish a body charged with affecting the problem of drug abuse and the crime related to it without providing even a nominal budget to facilitate its function.

8

The DEA, FBI, ATF, and All Those Other Acronyms

THE FEDS

The federal bureaus that are charged with law enforcement functions are of varied size and organization. Each is housed within whatever department of the national government Congress has deemed appropriate. Thus, the Federal Bureau of Investigation (FBI) is located in the Justice Department and the Bureau of Alcohol, Tobacco, and Firearms (ATF) is housed within the Department of the Treasury. The Secret Service is part of the Treasury Department also but has a mission much different from that of the ATF. Like the FBI, the Drug Enforcement Administration (DEA) belongs to the Department of Justice. It has a far more narrow mandate than the FBI, however, in that it is restricted to matters concerning drugs. At the same time, the charge of the DEA is broader than that of the FBI because it is as much a regulatory agency as it is a police entity. The Compliance Division of the DEA is essentially devoted to the civil regulation of doctors, pharmacies, and drug manufacturers.

There is a cornucopia of enforcement bureaus within the machinery of the federal government. There are even special agents who operate within the Department of Agriculture and are engaged in such esoteric pursuits as undercover food stamp sting operations. Such operatives have been known to enlist the aid of local police authorities for their investigations. I have loaned Agriculture agents listening devices to enable them to record black market transactions involving diverted food stamps. The Coast Guard, one might be surprised to find, is a part of the Department of Transportation, yet it is charged with everything from counting the number of seat cushions on boats to fighting wars in the deserts of the Middle East. There is also the Criminal Investigations Division of the Internal Revenue Service (CID), the Office of Special Investigations (OSI) located within the United States Air Force, and the U.S. Marshals' Service.

Congress has created law enforcement bureaus to meet every policing need it has seen fit to engage, each with its own charge and its own turf to protect. Like state and local police departments, the many enforcement bureaus of the U.S. government have often found themselves isolated from and at cross-purposes with their counterparts. This has resulted in a lack of coordination and even in a state of mutual distrust and acrimony. It is not for the purpose of expressing an endearment, after all, that many of the special agents of the DEA refer to their counterparts in the FBI as "feebs." Nor is it out of a desire to ease the burden of the FBI that the Bureau of Alcohol, Tobacco, and Firearms has lobbied for legislation designed to put it in charge of the federal anti-gang effort.

Like the smaller police bureaucracies of the states and their subordinate counties and municipalities, the federal bureaus are busy with the art of survival. Like other bureaucracies the FBI, ATF, IRS, and DEA seek to continue their existence and to grow in both size and scope. Thus, they are in competition with each other for a slice of the ever shrinking budget pie. And, like the prisons of Stojkovic' and Lovell's paper on corrections and the police departments that Perrow contends are primarily engaged in the preservation of form, the federal bureaus will do whatever it takes to survive and expand. It is little wonder, then, that once again the target is missed.

DÉJÀ VU

Just what is the target, then? What is the mark that is pursued instead? To address these two questions, we will first examine the situations of three of the nation's highest profile enforcement bureaus. The resulting analysis will ring familiar.

The FBI is relied upon as the principal law enforcement arm of the federal government. It has a broad mission of enforcing federal criminal statutes and is responsible for providing leadership and support to state and local police authorities. Examples of how it aids local police are its jurisdiction over interstate fugitives and bank robbery investigations, as well as its role as a clearinghouse for information and fingerprint records. The federal executive uses the FBI as its primary investigative arm, employing the bureau not only as a crime fighter but also as the vanguard of domestic counterintelligence. Even routine investigations, such as preappointment background searches, are conducted by the FBI.

The Drug Enforcement Administration is the agency of the Department of Justice that is charged with the regulation of the drug industry and the enforcement of the federal criminal statutes relating to dangerous drugs. Doctors, pharmacists, dentists, and pharmaceutical companies, as well as drug traffickers and street-level pushers, fall under the jurisdiction of the DEA. This particular agency of the Justice Department came into existence relatively recently, created by the Comprehensive Drug Abuse Prevention and Control Act of 1970. Prior to the passage of this act, the Bureau of Narcotics and Dangerous Drugs, the Office of Drug Abuse Law Enforcement, the Office of National Narcotics Intelligence, and the Bureau of Customs were responsible for such matters. Subsequent to the merger involving these entities, the division of criminal and civil responsibility within the DEA was accomplished by the creation of separate enforcement and compliance sections.

The DEA is able to function worldwide (unlike the FBI which shares its counter-intelligence function with the Central Intelligence Agency). Special Agents of the DEA are found in the jungles of Bolivia as well as in the urban environment of Mexico City, working with local authorities–and often local armies–to counter the production and exportation of illicit drugs. Until the late 1980s the FBI was not empowered to enforce the statutes that criminalize the sale and possession of cocaine, marijuana, and other illicit drugs. Previously, that function was the exclusive purview of the DEA and the states.

The ATF is, as noted earlier, a bureau of the Department of the Treasury. Like the DEA, the Bureau of Alcohol, Tobacco, and Firearms is both a police entity and a regulatory agency. Its mission is more complex than that of the DEA, however, because it deals not only with regulated substances such as beer, liquor, and tobacco but also with the manufacture, sale, possession, and trafficking of guns and ammunition. As we will see, still more turf has been carved out by the administrators of the ATF by virtue of its role in "gun-related crimes."

The FBI, then, is the nation's crime fighter, spy catcher, and principal investigative arm of the executive. The DEA is charged with protecting the citizenry from drug abuse and illicit trafficking of banned substances. The ATF would appear to be a cousin to the IRS that has taken on a larger role than the simple enforcement of industrial taxation. Why, then, has the FBI failed to hold its dominance over such matters as organized crime, and why has the ATF has taken a leadership position when it comes to combating street gangs in America? The answer to these questions can be summed up in a single word imperialism.

Matthew Holden, Jr., has written on how bureaucrats go about carving out turf and defending it in his paper "'Imperialism' in Bureaucracy."[1] Further, he points out that government bureaus raid the jurisdictions of other bureaus and departments in order to be in a position to deliver resources to their constituencies and so as to attract new constituent groups. Administrative politicians[2] seek the power that a broadened jurisdiction will provide in order to increase the size of their bureau and ensure its survival. Thus, the ATF has embraced the role of investigating drug related crimes such as delivery of cocaine while possessing a gun and using a handgun while committing a gang-related offense.

By taking on the added missions of eradicating gangs and deterring drug traffickers through the creative application of equally creative legislation, the ATF has moved into a position to compete with the FBI and the DEA for appropriations which are earmarked for organized crime and drug trafficking. The Bureau of Alcohol, Tobacco, and Firearms has thereby justified not only its existence, but also its expansion. Nothing enhances the power and prestige of an administrator like budget and jurisdictional authority.

Such tactics are commonplace in the arena of bureaucratic politics. The authors of the book *Organization Theory: A Public Perspective* point this out in their discussion of how administrators go about influencing goal-making policy. They illustrate how such executives become involved in the many means-ends conflicts[3] that arise from the debate between interest groups and politicians as they work to evolve a given policy such as law enforcement jurisdiction. They write, "Through reports, studies, recommendations, and other forms of information, bureaus may play a role in shaping policy."[4] Indeed, government bureaus use whatever means they have to promote themselves and expand the scope of the organization. By co-opting client constituencies as well as political allies, the various agencies and bureaus bring whatever influence they can generate to bear on the policymakers who decide their fate via appropriations bills. It is the nature of the beast.

The result of all of this is that the current federal arena strongly resembles the milieu of narcotics units and detective bureaus that predated the implementation of A-MEG. They are decentralized, overlapping, uncoordinated, and at cross-purposes. Not surprisingly, the federal organizations have begun to employ a strategy similar to the metropolitan enforcement groups in an effort to overcome this. Federal task forces are now trendy and fashionable, and although they have been in existence since the 1970s,[5] they are far more numerous than ever before. There are federal drug task forces, federal anti-gang task forces, and federal fugitive task forces. Within these multijurisdictional groups are agents of the ATF, FBI, DEA, IRS, and U.S. Marshals. Many include local police detectives and state investigators.

The theory, of course is the same for the federal task forces as it is for the metropolitan enforcement groups. The pooling of resources is expected to result in a synergistic effect with regard to such matters as specialized expertise, economies of scale, manpower availability, centralized command, intelligence sharing, and improved coordination. Yet street violence, gun crimes, and drug trafficking go on unabated—year after year. Innovative programs, such as the ATF's Operation Triggerlock (an effort that targeted gun offenders by emphasizing arrests for gun crimes resulting in mandatory prison sentences), wax and wane. Triggerlock, an initiative that was popular under the Bush administration, has been eliminated under President Clinton. And just as it complained about the flood of defendants clogging the courts on "petty" drug charges, the federal judiciary has now complained of the unreasonable burden the Triggerlock program has placed on its dockets.

I do not intend to revisit the story of A-MEG via the current situation in the federal task force frenzy. Rather, I point it out only to make the reader aware that the use of myths and symbols is not the exclusive property of local politicians and administrators. It should be noted, however, that such as this has been tried before at the federal level of government-and failed.

In response to an initiative by Presdent Johnson, the Buffalo Strike Force was created in 1967.[6] In a push to make headway against organized crime, Johnson charged his administration, and especially the Justice Department, with implementing a coordinated attack on the underworld. Under the auspices of the Organized Crime and Racketeering Section of that department, a large number of federal agencies combined resources. These included the Bureau of Customs, the IRS, the Bureau of Narcotics and Dangerous Drugs, the ATF, and others. Even the Royal Canadian Mounted Police were on board. This experiment met with some early success, and the concept was quickly expanded. The number of such task forces grew to thirteen by 1977.[7]

At about the same time the Safe Streets Act was enacted with much fanfare. It was an important part of the Johnson administration's plan for dealing with rising crime, and a key component of the bill was the creation of the Law Enforcement Assistance Administration (LEAA).[8] LEAA was intended to be a central coordinator of the federal anti-crime effort. It was to oversee federal funding of state and local law enforcement efforts as well as to supervise anti-crime planning. In addition, LEAA was to provide support and guidance to municipal and state police agencies, and to the government subdivisions that had jurisdiction over them. To serve as the interface between the federal bureaucracy and that of the states, counterparts to the LEAA were created in each state. These new state bureaus were to oversee the distribution of funds to the municipalities and serve as offices for reviewing anti-crime planning by the cities and counties.

In their book *U.S. v. Crime in the Streets*, Thomas E. Cronin, Tania Z. Cronin, and Michael E. Milakovich note that during its twelve-year history, the LEAA was touted both by the Johnson and the Nixon administrations as a key component in the effective attack on crime.[9] It had been brought into existence in 1968 by legislation aggressively supported by President Johnson. Nixon also made use of its appeal once he took office. On page 83 of their book, Cronin, et al. write, "Attorney General John Mitchell was on record as saying that no issue was more important than crime for the Justice Department and that no administration program had higher priority than LEAA."[10] The rhetoric was indeed on the side of an intense, federally coordinated national anti-crime program.

It would seem to even a somewhat skeptical observer that the federal government had declared all-out war on crime. But careful scrutiny of the realities reveals yet another well-orchestrated scam. In 1977 the Office of the Comptroller General of the United States released a report to the Congress titled *War On Organized Crime Faltering -- Federal Strike Forces Not Getting the Job Done*.[11] Released some ten years after the Buffalo Strike Force had come into being, the report concluded that the ballyhooed federal strike forces had struck out in the battle to reduce organized crime. It coldly lists the reasons for the failure, which by now should sound frighteningly familiar:

–The Government still has not developed a strategy to fight organized crime.
–There is no agreement on what organized crime is and, consequently, on precisely whom or what the Government is fighting.
–The strike forces have no statement of objectives or plans for achieving those objectives.
–Individual strike forces are hampered because the Justice attorneys-in-charge have no authority over participants from other agencies.
–No system exists for evaluating the effectiveness of the national effort or of individual strike forces.
–A costly computerized organized crime intelligence system is, as the Department of Justice agrees, of dubious value.

Just as A-MEG, at the local level, was unable to gain control of itself, so it was with the strike forces. Confused systems of authority, a lack of coordination, and poor information flow are the culprits here as well. Yet, again in the 1980s and 1990s the federal task force is a prime mechanism of the federal effort against organized crime and drug trafficking. It has even become trendy to attack such mundane problems as serving fugitive warrants via the mechanism of federally led task force operations. One is compelled to ask why such policies persist.

The history of the LEAA provides a hint as to why task force operations remain in vogue, for it paints a picture of the political commitment of the federal government in the war on crime that mirrors that of the implementers of the A-MEG program covered in chapter 4. With the rise of the federal strike force came a concomitant rise in the salience of the LEAA, but as Cronin et al. point out, the agency's importance was far more flash than substance.

The LEAA, Cronin et al. report, was created by passage of the 1968 Safe Streets Act as the result of political pressure to attack the crime problem at the national level.[12] The authors note that the federal government proceeded to take over the campaign against crime even though there was little hard knowledge of how to go about it.[13] Not only the fact that they faced a large unknown—crime reduction—hampered policymakers; a lack of experience with the block grant mechanism used to fund it was an obstacle as well.[14] What resulted was ambiguous and unstable legislation and policy—and, in the end, failure. "The Safe Streets Act was amended five times," they write, "basically each time it came up for reauthorization (until finally planning and action funds were totally cut out of the budget, reducing the Law Enforcement Assistance Administration to a skeletal administrative operation in 1981)."[15]

Just as was discovered during the case study of A-MEG, Cronin et al. find that political will for supporting the stated agenda of the LEAA was anything but commensurate with the passionate rhetoric of the age. They write of how needed funding changes were enacted in "an unsystematic and 'Band-Aid' manner (until the final amendments in 1979, which completely reorganized the agency but which were followed by no appropriations for LEAA grants)."[16] Philosophic differences plagued the agency, and as administrations changed, so did the thrust and leadership of the LEAA—when it was not left vacant by a less than committed president. The authors observe that when Charles Rogovin resigned as the administrator for LEAA in 1970 the office was left vacant for nine months by President Nixon.[17] Here again we see that actions belie any proclamation that a war on crime is being waged.

Just as it has served the maintenance of the status quo among the states and their political subdivisions, so the facade of multijurisdictional effort serves to create the illusion that Washington is determined to eradicate organized crime and gangs. One finds upon close examination, however, that the campaigns are only the recounted tales of a now ancient myth. Actions will always betray intent, and it has become painfully obvious that the national government is not all that serious about crime and violence. It is serious about image, however, as politicians have always been. It is the legend, then, that concerns them most, as are the myths and symbols that support it.

A DIFFERENT ORDER OF MAGNITUDE

A more accurate picture of what is occurring can be gained by examining the distribution of resources in the fight against drugs and violence. Let us look into the orders of magnitude concerning this issue by comparing the financing of the war on crime with a few of the other popular campaigns that have been waged by our government. Take the Persian Gulf War, for example. Jean Edward Smith summarizes the overall effort of the conflict on page 9 of his book titled *George Bush's War*.[18] The United States deployed 540,000 troops to fight in Operation Desert Storm and exploded "142,000 tons of bombs"[19] during the war. The entire war was over in forty-three days. The battle on the ground lasted only 100 hours; 148 of our troops were killed. The total cost of the war was about $40 billion, much of which was subsidized by our allies. It should be noted, however, that the United States forgave the Egyptian war debt—an amount totalling 7.1 billion—and other pledges were not exactly forthcoming after the fighting was over.

The Vietnam War was another conflict in which America took on a wartime role. At its height, there were about 500,000 U.S. troops deployed in southeast

Asia in support of that military action. By 1967 the war was estimated to cost the U.S. taxpayers about $25 billion annually.[20] America fought that war for more than a decade and lost more than 50,000 lives to the cause of maintaining the borders of South Vietnam.

When we speak of the great wars, we enter into a whole new order of magnitude. Here we will discuss the costs in terms of a percentage of GNP.[21] In his book *The Line of Fire*, the former chairman of the Joint Chiefs of Staff, Admiral William J. Crowe, Jr., points out that at the end of 1991, the United States was spending between 4 and 5 percent of its GNP on defense.[22] He makes clear how dramatic World War II really was, pointing out that during that war the nation spent about 35 percent of GNP on the military.[23] The Korean conflict took some 20 percent, and the Vietnam War used up about 8 or 9 percent of the nation's productivity. The reader can gain some perspective on this in terms of dollars through the fact that the total military budget of the United States in the current era tends to run about $300 billion dollars annually.[24]

One can also draw some insight from comparing the effort expended on the drug war with what has been invested into yet another well-known "war"— the war on poverty. In 1964 President Lyndon Johnson declared a war on poverty and outlined his vision for a Great Society in which America would seek to ease the plight of the nation's poor. Since that initial declaration Johnson and his successors have presided over the expenditure of trillions of dollars in an effort to achieve victory. Hundreds of billions of dollars are committed each year in the continuing fight to raise the poor to a reasonable standard of living. No end is yet in sight to what at times seems to be an insoluble problem; yet, having created a number of institutions and programs devoted to the anti-poverty effort, America continues to be committed to this noble cause.

How then, does the effort to fight crime in America measure up to the other great battles we have fought, and continue to fight? More specifically, how does the war on drugs stack up against them? According to the federal government's Bureau of Justice Statistics (BJS), local police departments spent $20.6 billion in 1992 and employed about 363,000 sworn officers. Sheriff's departments spent about $9.1 billion during the same period and had about 141,000 such personnel. State police units account for about another $3.7 billion in spending and approximately 52,000 law enforcement officers. All told, about $33.4 billion was spent at the state and local level for police services and some 556,000 peace officers were engaged in the business of public safety.

For the federal drug war we find a much smaller set of figures. Let us look at the total Justice Department budget for 1993. It is this department that houses both the Federal Bureau of Investigation and the Drug Enforcement Administration. According to the BJS, the total budget for 1993 at the Justice Department was $11.3 billion. This is not only the dollars used for operating the department's own divisions and bureaus, but includes monies parceled out to state and local governments to run such programs as the Weed and Seed Program (a project that targets certain dangerous offenders, increases police visibility, and pursues neighborhood restoration programs). It is noteworthy that specialized grant programs designed to augment local police in the implementation of such projects as metropolitan enforcement groups and cannabis suppression are measured in the millions, rather than the billions, of dollars.

When one compares these figures, an all too vivid picture of the war on drugs begins to emerge. When one considers that less is spent annually on the total of police services in the United States ($33.4 billion) than was expended in the brief Persian Gulf War (about $40 billion), one begins to realize that the war on drugs is just another scam. Even if the total Justice Department budget of $11.3 billion is added in the whole amount only barely squeaks past at $44.7 billion. In fact, one estimate puts the total of all federal, state, and local law enforcement budgets at only $39 billion.[25] Figure 8.1 compares the budgets of the police, the Justice Department, the Vietnam War, and the Persian Gulf War. Remember, also, that drug enforcement accounts for only a small portion of what the police do. By far, the average police officer spends his or her time answering service calls rather than fighting crime. Most estimates put the percentage of time spent by a police officer in responding to crimes at 10 to 20 percent.

FIGURE 8.1

Budgets for State and Local Police, the Department of Justice, the Gulf War, and the Vietnam War (billions of dollars)

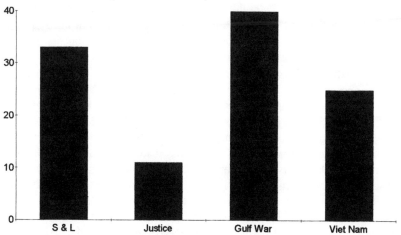

THE STATUS QUO REVISITED

Not only is it not very likely that federal programs have done much to augment state and local drug enforcement efforts, but it is more accurate to state that the federal agencies are dwarfed by the latter. The few thousand DEA agents scattered around the globe could never hope to impact on the domestic drug trafficking program alone, and the same goes for the FBI's complement of personnel. As for the ATF, it has its hands full administering its regulatory duties connected with weapons dealers, breweries, and tobacco manufactures.

As an alternative, the federal authorities have sought to co-opt the local police through the encouragement of joint efforts, in the form of the federal task force and of metropolitan enforcement groups. Yet, even using this tactic, the number of officers and agents who serve on most such teams can be counted on one's fingers and toes. Often, they are underequipped and need to borrow such things as listening devices and surveillance vans from the local departments on an ad hoc and as-available basis.

The federal agencies, as anxious to justify their existence as any other bureaucracy, attempt to engender cooperation with the sheriff's departments and other local police services in any way they can, and they can be quite creative in finding a niche that only they can fill. One such effort that was particularly successful in gaining acceptance with local law enforcement but is of somewhat dubious value is known as the Cannabis Enforcement and Suppression Effort (CEASE). It may well be considered a bit of marketing genius. In this program the DEA provides funding (in the hundreds of thousands of dollars) to the various states that buy into the program and agree to administer it. Out of this, the National Guard is provided with monies to operate helicopters and ground units for ferrying "specially trained spotters" who have been schooled in the identification of marijuana from the air. The spotters are local police officers who are sent to a special school to become "experts" in the aerial identification of marijuana plants.

I was chosen to be one of those spotters during the late 1980s. It was great sport. During the course of the marijuana growing season, flights were scheduled over the area of my jurisdiction, and I would take off from the local airport in one of the Guard's Hueys or Bell choppers to scan for plots of marijuana. Ground teams would wait in the search area, and I would direct them to various locations where it appeared that contraband might be found.

We burned hundreds of thousands of marijuana plants during the three years I was assigned to the CEASE program. Most of them, however, were wild hemp, a low-grade cannabis that was produced on local farms for making rope during World War II. Still, it looked good on paper, and the feds wanted it destroyed. Only a few hundred plants were of the potent variety of marijuana, such as *Cannabis sativa*.

Here again we find the employment of myths and symbols where concrete progress is either out of reach or never intended. Any number of such projects can be cited. The federal bureaus have employed many with such monikers as "highway interdiction," a program involving the detection of drug courier cars along interstate highway routes and other common overland corridors, and the "asset forfeiture program," which allowed local police to seize drug-related assets under federal administrative authority. Such programs appeal to local law enforcement because they tend to bring overtime funding and usable assets, such as undercover cars and cash that can be used to pay informants. The obvious appeal of the CEASE project is that the police got to use military helicopters and obtain specialized training. There is nothing like helicopter rides and an expanded resume' to win over an ally in the local narcotics unit. Everyone comes out ahead. The federal agencies that fund the program win a much-needed ally and the personnel who come with it. The local police department obtains a great deal of good press and increased prestige. The drug traffickers, no doubt, take great solace in the knowledge that the police are diverting considerable resources to such concerns as eradicating wild hemp. The only loser is the public.

Once again, I wish to stress how important it is not to overstate the case being made here. As was noted in chapter 2 it is not the intent of this book to allege some overarching conspiracy to avoid enforcing the criminal statutes. The director of the FBI and his counterparts in the DEA and ATF are not on a mission to ensure the continued flow of drugs into the United States any more than the penitentiary system is working to flood our neighborhoods with dangerous felons. Unintended and damaging consequences often result from flawed decision making simply because administrative politicians rationalize away the fact that they are acting out of self-interest rather than the public interest. Flawed thinking, or perhaps a weakened sense of duty, accounts for far more of this type of phenomenon than does criminal malfeasance.

By way of illustration I offer an account of a conversation I had with one of the students currently enrolled in my criminology class. During the course of a lecture this very question came up, and the exchange between student and teacher was quite informative. This particular student is a seventeen-year veteran police officer with a great deal of experience as a homicide detective and a narcotics investigator. In trying to understand how the police can fall into the trap of enabling drug kingpins to operate with impunity, we examined the detective's own experience in narcotics enforcement. When asked what most occupied his time while working narcotics the officer, conceded that serving search warrants on drug houses and making covert drug buys from street dealers made up the bulk of his fieldwork. When asked why he did not spend more time making cases against drug kingpins and their lieutenants he stated that they were extremely difficult to outmaneuver, the process being a long-term and labor-intensive one. In the end, we agreed that the police, like any other entity, will follow the path of least resistance—the road most traveled. The reason for this, of course, is that a police unit can rack up a lot of arrests by crashing down drug house doors and picking up street dealers. It looks good on paper and is easy to accomplish. Narcotics units also can generate a good deal of press on a regular basis in this way. There is little incentive to target the top of a cocaine ring and spend months, even years, dismantling his or her operation and painstakingly gathering evidence to indict on conspiracy charges.

It can again be seen here that truly bizarre themes can arise out of the interplay of politics and administration. The very machinery that we have put into place to eradicate organized crime and the importation of drugs has been distracted from that goal. Oddly, it has led itself astray or has allowed itself to be diverted by the petty interests of bureaucratic politics. The winner, of course, is the status quo.

NOTES

1. Matthew Holden, Jr., "'Imperialism' in Bureaucracy," in *Bureaucratic Power in National Policy Making*, ed. Francis E. Rourke (Boston, 1986), 28-44.
2. Ibid., 29.
3. Harold F. Gortner, Julianne Mahler, and Jeanne Bell Nicholson, *Organization Theory: A Public Perspective* (Chicago, 1987), 36.
4. Ibid., 36.
5. Jan Chaiken, Marcia Chaiken, and Clifford Karchmer, *Multijurisdictional Drug Law Enforcement Strategies: Reducing Supply and Demand* (Washington, DC, 1990).
6. *Report of the National Conference on Organized Crime* (Washington, DC, 1975), 36.
7. *War on Organized Crime Faltering—Federal Strike Forces Not Getting the Job Done* (Washington, DC, 1977), i.
8. Thomas E. Cronin, Tania Z. Cronin, and Michael E. Milakovich, *U.S. v. Crime in the Streets* (Bloomington, IN, 1981), 79.
9. Ibid., 77-86.
10. Ibid., 83.
11. *War On Organized Crime Faltering*, i.
12. Cronin et al, 77.
13. Ibid., 78.
14. Ibid., 79-80.
15. Ibid., 78.

16. Ibid., 78.

17. Ibid., 84.

18. Jean Edward Smith, *George Bush's War* (New York, 1992), 9.

19. Ibid., 9.

20. *Funk and Wagnells New Encyclopedia* (1983), vol. 27, 57.

21. Although we now measure national productivity as Gross Domestic Product, during the time of the wars being examined, the term was Gross National Product. We will use this latter designation.

22. Admiral William J. Crowe, Jr., *The Line of Fire* (New York, 1993), 331.

23. Ibid.

24. Ibid., 232.

25. "Violent Crime," *U.S. News & World Report*, January 17, 1994, 40-41.

9

Army, Navy, Air Force, and Marines?

The police and federal law enforcement authorities are not the only departments of government that find themselves misused by the trendy rhetoric of the drug war. The Department of Defense has not escaped the call to arms being issued by politicians in their rush to impress the citizenry with their zeal to rid our streets of violence and drugs. The traditional turf of state bureaus of investigation and local police have been invaded by machete-wielding National Guardsmen sent to chop down marijuana fields as well as by military intelligence analysts deployed to assist drug enforcement task forces in targeting drug traffickers. The Navy is now involved in the tracking of vessels suspected of carrying heroin, cocaine, and other illicit drugs, an area normally the purview of the Coast Guard, the Bureau of Customs, and the DEA. Whether on the ground, in the air, or on the open seas, our military services are charged with the interdiction and suppression of illegal drugs.

The wisdom of pressing the military into police duties is worth questioning, however, on several fronts. Political implications abound in such an arrangement. The whole idea of maintaining a police force separate from that of the military is predicated on the need for a free society to be in control of its own civil government. The U.S. military has been carefully relegated to a strict role of defense and foreign operations. Only in extreme emergencies, such as during hurricanes and large floods, is the military called into the otherwise civilian-led concern of public safety. Of course, one might argue that the current drug crisis is such an emergency, but will that argument stand on the merits? Does the use of military units make sense in light of their traditional missions and expertise? Have all other means been tried, short of risking the establishment of a police state?

THE ROLE OF THE MILITARY

Vice Admiral William P. Mack and Navy Captain Thomas D. Paulsen delineate the functions and duties of the U.S. Navy in their book, *The Naval Officer's Guide.*[1] They write that the Department of the Navy is responsible for such functions as preparing the Marines Corps and Navy to make them capable of the "effective prosecution of war," "the seizure or defense of advanced naval bases," "furnish[ing] adequate, timely, and reliable intelligence for the Navy and Marine Corps," and "provid[ing] air support essential for naval operations."[2] The list of functions is, of course, longer than this short example, but nowhere do the authors indicate that the Navy is charged with either interdicting shipments of heroin and cocaine or shadowing drug couriers. They make it quite plain that the National Security Act does not focus on such law enforcement duties but, rather, is concerned with the defense of the United States from foreign enemies.

One finds that the mission of the U.S. Army is no more compatible with crime fighting than that of the Navy. Lieutenant Colonel Lawrence P. Crocker wrote the *Army Officer's, Guide* and in it he explains the objective or purpose of the Army.[3] He points out that it is set in place by Title 10 of the United States Code and that it includes such functions as "the effective prosecution of war," "preserving the peace and security," and "overcoming any nations responsible for aggressive acts."[4] Again, this is only a representative list, but it accurately portrays the Army as the combat-oriented department that it is. It is not a law enforcement agency.

One must concede, certainly, that the phrase "preserving the peace and security" does open the door a little for justifying use of the Army when civil order breaks down. Presidents have done so. Who can forget the site of Army jeeps bearing sky-mounted machine guns and streams of troop transports rolling into the cities during the riots of the late 1960s. Yet instances such as those occurred during extraordinary circumstances when the police were not capable of restoring order to a level that would allow for such critical services such fire fighting and emergency rescue. The cities were burning, and the police were powerless to stop it. Once calm had returned to the point where the fire rigs could roll in and extinguish flames and it was safe for the police to resume routine patrols, the army withdrew. Quickly, the troops were returned to their barracks.

As for that modern-day militia, the National Guard, reliance on the citizen soldier holds little more merit. Samuel Walker makes this clear in his policy guide titled *Sense and Nonsense About Crime and Drugs.* He points out that citizen soldiers are not trained in law enforcement techniques, nor are they schooled in constitutional and criminal law. He reminds us also that the National Guard is not accountable to civilian officials.[5] Those who are calling for the National Guard to patrol the streets are well advised to consider the fact that no mayor or county executive can call up a military field commander and order him or her to change tactics or withdraw from a given locale. To quote Walker, "And do we really want a permanent military occupation of our cities?"[6] From my own perspective, the supposed wisdom of using National Guard troops can be debunked by the utterance of just two words: Kent State.

LEAVE IT TO THE COAST GUARD

Why, then, have many determined that our best hope for winning the battle against the drug cartels lies in the mobilization of the U.S. Military? Has the Coast Guard fallen short? Perhaps. But why?

It seems odd that the government is willing to alter the role of the Department of Defense and divert its assets to a law enforcement function rather than simply augment the resources of the U.S. Coast Guard. The Coast Guard has both a tradition of law enforcement and the training to do the job well. Its ocean craft are better suited to such a mission, and its officers and enlisted personnel are oriented to the task. It is the specialty of this branch of the services to protect our coastal waters—it is their turf. They, along with the Bureau of Customs and the Border Patrol are our front line of defense in such matters. As regards the importation of illicit drugs, the ranks of the above agencies have been augmented by the Drug Enforcement Administration. Why not bolster these agencies with additional equipment and personnel rather than divert vital assets of defense?

What better benefit could be garnered from the so-called peace dividend than ensuring the security of our borders against illicit drugs and the traffickers who facilitate their importation? Who is better trained and more experienced in the task than the Coast Guard and its companion agencies of the departments of the Treasury and Justice? It would seem logical that an infusion of new boats and planes into these services, an upgrading of detection systems, and an increase in personnel in their respective staffs could reap profoundly higher rates of return than co-optation of the Army, Navy, or Air Force. As they say in the popular culture, "It's a no brainer!"

At best, law enforcement is interdicting 5 to 10 percent of the drugs being smuggled into the United States. It has been documented in this book that the budget devoted to the war on crime is puny in comparison with those of our other wars, both military and social. This state of affairs would seem to contradict the trendy rhetoric that we are engaged in an all-out campaign to eradicate drug trafficking and the crime it inspires. And the claim that concern with retaining the traditions of an open society has tended to preclude such a self-imposed blockade of our shores, rings hollow when we have ordered our own Navy to tighten such a noose—or have we?

There is no evidence that drug smuggling is being impacted by the conscription of our military into the war on drugs. Certainly we can conclude that it is not grinding to a halt. If the military wishes to stop a smuggling operation, it has the means to do so. The Navy simply institutes a blockade, turning back some vessels and boarding others. The Army seals off borders and searches all who cross. The Air Force takes command of the skies. And when the Department of Defense so acts, it does it in force. Our armed forces by and large are not trained in crime detection and issues of probable cause. They act in the fashion such organizations are designed to do. The minor support that the military services can offer to law enforcement (on an as-available basis) is more in the area of tracking and intelligence—and this is of questionable compatibility with the needs of the police.

Why, then, has the government chosen to order the military into that theater of battle known popularly as the war on drugs? I submit that it is for the same reasons that the municipal leaders who founded A-MEG elected to turn over local drug enforcement duties to a multijurisdictional task force: so they could claim that they were doing something about crime and drugs. Never mind that funding for the unit was minuscule. Never mind the reality that virtually every initiative A-MEG undertook was a failure. Local politicians could point to A-MEG and claim that they were at the cutting edge of leadership when it came to fighting crime.

The only way that choosing to order in the military rather than properly funding the Coast Guard and its traditional allies makes sense is if you orient your thinking in much the same way that we did in our analysis of the motives of the implememters and politicians of A-MEG. It is just another scam. It is an easy solution to a political dilemma. No hard decisions about where to get the money need be made by the politicians faced with the problem of confronting the smugglers. The Department of Defense has an enormous budget, and hundreds of ships and aircraft on patrol around the world. The pretense that the efforts of law enforcement can be enhanced by including the military in an overall program of surveillance and interdiction is an easy one to set up without raising taxes or fighting an appropriations battle. After all, it looks good on paper.

STATING THE OBVIOUS

Once again we find that the war on crime and drugs is best understood when it is viewed as just another scam. We will not find salvation in the arms of the military. We will never find security in the form of a ready-made panacea. The only way to deal with the problem of drugs in American society is to confront it head-on. In Part III the "how" of this will be examined. For now, suffice it to say that when it comes to fighting the smugglers on the open seas, leave it to the Coast Guard.

NOTES

1. William P. Mack and Thomas D. Paulsen, *The Naval Officer's Guide* (Annapolis, 1983), 299-302.

2. Ibid.

3. Lawrence P. Crocker, *Army Officer's Guide* (Harrisburg, PA: Stackpole Books, 1990), p. 468.

4. Ibid.

5. Samuel Walker, *Sense and Nonsense About Crime and Drugs* (Belmont, CA: Wadsworth, 1994), p. 12.

6. Ibid.

Part III

THE CHALLENGE

10

The Hobbesian World of the Modern Age

In chapter 5 I wrote of the existence of an undeclared armistice between law enforcement and the criminal element. As was noted, it is an unspoken truce, so no mechanisms have been put into place for monitoring the arrangement. There are no independent peacekeepers to oversee the demilitarized zones. Rather, they have been self-policed, and so long as it was in the mutual interest of all the parties to the agreement to practice restraint, the tacit understanding held. But the reader may have noticed that, of late, there have been certain unseemly breaches of the peace in the traditional cease-fire zones.

Our schools and marketplaces, and even the open streets, have begun to lose the civil character of a modern society. And the violence has progressed to the point where not a single home or open park can be claimed as a safe haven from the carnage that rocks our communities. There is no last bastion of retreat. The war of all against all has returned once again in all its fury. That which was posited as a theoretical construct by political philosophers such as Thomas Hobbes has burst upon the present age with a terrifying concreteness. One should never forget the lessons taught in Hobbes's *Leviathan* for though it may be a theoretical abstraction, the impact of the state of nature on the condition of human society is very real. Yet, it appears that we have either abandoned or lost sight of the reasoning of Hobbes. Indeed, it would seem that we have rejected the common philosophy of community.

Some readers might think the assertion that traditional order has broken down is an overstatement. That being the case, they will most certainly regard the contention that such a breakdown is the direct result of that same traditional order to be absurd. Yet that is exactly the contention of this book. Let us proceed.

CRISIS YET AGAIN

First, the case must be made that we are indeed in crisis, for there are some who would claim that we are not. In Great Britain a very famous, if not infamous, phrase was first uttered in 1971 by Home Secretary Reginald Maulding when he spoke of "an acceptable level of violence"[1] in regard to the conflict in Northern Ireland. It was his belief that the Irish Republican Army's deadly attacks could be "reduced to an acceptable level."[2] Thus, the political status quo could continue without the need for England to drastically change its policies concerning the status of Northern Ireland. Since the imposition in 1972[3] of direct British rule through the Northern Ireland Office, 2400 people have been killed in violence related to the conflict between England and the IRA.[4] Between 1973 and 1985 there were 1,110 kneecappings[5] (a procedure wherein the IRA shoots a bullet through the legs or knees of the unfortunate who crosses them). Terrorist bombs have periodically been set off in Northern Ireland and England. Between 1971 and 1985 an average of 25 British soldiers were killed each year in the civil war in Northern Ireland.[6] Assassination has taken the life of both the common subject and the lofty noble. Yet England, by its willingness to endure these casualties, has affirmed Maulding's assertion that there is an acceptable level of violence.

This being the case, one might ask how serious can the situation really be in the United States? Certainly such a thinker might note that if a society can continue to function with a casualty rate of 56 per year, as is the case in Northern Ireland–a country of only 1.5 million people–then certainly America can move forward unhindered. As it happens, however, our casualty rates are much higher than those of the Irish. There are 24,700 homicides annually in the United States, a rate that roughly matches the total loss of US troops in the Vietnam war every two years.[7] At the height of the war between England and the IRA, the casualty rate reached a total of 467 for a single year. Individual cities in this country routinely experience homicide levels that rival this figure,[8] and homicide is a leading cause of death of young black males. The annual homicide rate for New York City alone exceeds 2,000, very nearly matching the total number killed in the IRA's war with Great Britain.[9] The situation, then, is very serious.

Should one be tempted to minimize the figures cited above by asserting that they are incompatible with our own situation because the population of Northern Ireland is quite small, the notion is easily refuted when the numbers are converted into percentages. The death rate of 56 soldiers and civilians killed in the Anglo-Irish conflict represents about 0.0037 percent of the population of Ulster, while the 24,700 Americans who were homicide victims of homicides in 1991 account for approximately 0.0097 percent of the US population. Nearly three times as many Americans as British subjects then, are killed by their fellow citizens, when calculated on a percentage basis. To place this in context, one only need run the numbers. At a rate of 24,700 homicides per year, Americans will kill a number of their countrymen roughly equal to the population of the city of Baton Rouge in the next decade. Over the course of the next century they will eliminate a population matching that of the state of Arkansas. As one can readily see, we have arrived at the doorstep of a truly Hobbesian era in the history of our nation. Figure 10.1 depicts this graphically.

FIGURE 10.1
Number of Americans Who Die by Homicide Annually, by Decade, by 100 Years (in thousands)

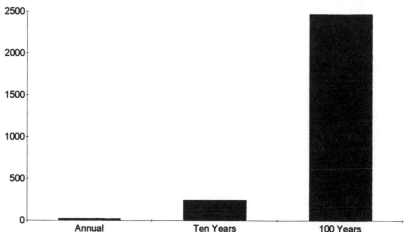

Still, it can be countered that commerce continues to thrive. Literature, art, and science still flourish. This is all true, and for some, we may still be at an acceptable level of violence. But history paints a harsher picture. Not only are Americans dying at the hands of other Americans in numbers rivaling those of modern civil wars, but they are being killed in numbers not reached in this century or the last.

In his paper "*Historical Trends in Violent Crime: A Critical Review of the Evidence*," Ted Robert Gurr drives home the reality that ours is perhaps the most violent era of our national history.[10] Certainly it is the most violent since before the Civil War. Gurr notes that there have been three great surges in violent crime since the 1840s. Violence in the early nineteenth century was, according to Gurr, "stable or declining," but surged dramatically "shortly before the Civil War and persisted into the 1870s."[11] Gurr points out that from 1900 to the 1930s a "sustained rise in violent crime" occurred.[12] Subsequent to this, the rate dropped for thirty years, only to rise dramatically until by 1980 it had reached an all-time high. Gurr writes: "Current national homicide rates are higher than any recorded previously, though only slightly greater than those of the 1920's."[13] Unfortunately, it does not seem likely that his last remark will hold for very long. Although the rate of homicides in the United States dropped from 10.2 per 100,000 inhabitants in 1980 to 7.9 in 1985, it had jumped to 10.0 by 1991, and the trend is definitely on the upswing.[14] Figures 10.2 and 10.3 illustrate this situation, using data provided by the U.S. Department of Justice.[15]

FIGURE 10.2
Homicides per 100,000 Population, 1900-1991

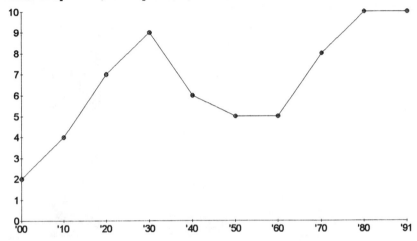

Source: U.S. Department of Justice.

Other writers have noted these same trends (Harries, 1990) and have attempted to explain their causes, examining such issues as race and immigration, and legal factors such as the enactment of prohibition.[16] Our purpose here is less ambitious. It is only to point out that ours is a less civilized time today than yesterday. Save for the outbreak of a major war, we will suffer no greater casualties than these. Indeed, claims by the politicians that we are faced with a threat tantamount to that of war seems to be supported by the evidence. It is remarkable, then, that a wartime effort has not truly been put into place.

FIGURE 10.3
Homicides per 100,000 Population, 1981-1991

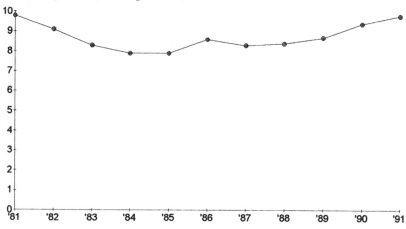

Source: U.S. Department of Justice

THE TRADITIONAL ORDER

It is here that the writing of Jeffrey H. Reiman becomes most helpful. According to Reiman, one can "make more sense out of criminal justice policy by assuming that its goal is to maintain crime than by assuming that its goal is to reduce crime!"[17] By this he means not that bureaucrats and politicians set out to maintain a high level of crime when enacting and implementing criminal justice policy, but that the clear result of the policies and programs that are in place has that effect. The violence and property crime that have plagued us throughout the decades examined in this book are *acceptable results as opposed to targeted goals*. None-the-less, those who govern must be regarded as responsible for failing to pursue more noble ends. There should be no "acceptable level of violence" from the perspective of public policy.

In his book *The Rich Get Richer and the Poor Get Prison* Jeffrey Reiman lays out his assertion that certain levels of street crime not only are acceptable but serve a useful function for the powerful elite of American society in the form of his "Pyrrhic defeat theory."[18] The opposite of a Pyrrhic victory, in which a military goal is achieved at such a terrible loss of life and resources as to amount to a defeat, the Pyrrhic defeat of Reiman's theory is one in which failure *is* the goal! The American criminal justice system is, for him, one that seeks to scapegoat the poor as the cause of crime-particularly street crime-in our communities. By holding up the underclass as the source of violent crime, those in power distract the public from the crimes of the elite. Such ills as white-collar-crime, abuse of employees by industry (e.g., requiring them to work in poorly ventilated coal mines), and deaths resulting from unnecessary surgery go unassailed. "Nothing succeeds like failure,"[19] writes Reiman, when it comes to hiding behind the problem of dangerous street crime.

The American system of justice is, for Reiman, like a carnival mirror[20] in that it reflects a distorted image of our society. As we look into our system of law enforcement, it reflects an image of society that we use to asses our circumstances and develop a perspective about ourselves and our fellows. Because it selectively focuses its attention on the poor and on the street crime that is so prevalent in their quarters while ignoring the crimes of the rich and powerful it reflects an image that is anything but true. The vision that meets us as we peer into the reflection is so inherently wrong that we are unable to use it effectively as a gauge of our progress as a nation. It is not a true representation of the condition of our times.

It is only natural, therefore, that those who *have* are in no great hurry to change things for the better. So far as the wealthy are concerned, the situation could not be much better. As for the middle class, so long as they can move safely to job and to school, and so long as they can enjoy the many parks and shopping districts of our cities and countrysides, they are satisfied. Except for the poor of this country, there would be virtually no clamor at all for change. For until now it has been only they who have lived in the kill zones of a nation supposedly at peace and only they who have suffered the casualties that litter the fields outside the demilitarized zones.   Up until now we have been experiencing what many had decided was an acceptable level of violence.

Yet it may be perhaps that the first signs of a major offensive are beginning to appear. In August of 1994 President Clinton was pleased to learn that the new Omnibus Crime Bill has been passed into law and that thousands of law enforcement officers for which he has called are now expected to become a reality. This will be a dramatic increase of the personnel devoted to policework within the United States. In my home state of Wisconsin there is a frenzy of legislative initiatives designed to fight violent crime. The result has been that here, as in other states, boot camps for repeat offenders have been instituted and new prisons have been built.   Only a few weeks ago Governor Tommy Thompson signed a "three strikes, you're out" bill into law; it requires that an offender convicted of a felony for the third time spend the rest of his or her life behind bars.

Everywhere in the media one reads and hears about the clamor for action and the shock of a nation that has discovered itself in crisis. Newspaper headlines have become a veritable ticker tape of violence. Television news is reminiscent of the body count reports in the days of the conflict in Vietnam. A cursory review of your local library's 1993 collection of *Time, Newsweek,* and *U. S. News & World Report* will yield no less than seven of those magazine covers devoted to crime and violence, and the stories inside them are alarming indeed. They speak of murders on the rise in our schools and violence so prevalent that, according to *Time,* "Gunshots now cause one of every four deaths among American teenagers."[21] In its November 8, 1993 issue *U.S. News & World Report* notes, alarmingly, that 10 percent of children admitted to the pediatric clinic of Boston City Hospital during the previous year had witnessed a stabbing or shooting by the time they had reached the age of six.[22] And in an article entitled, "Danger in the Safety Zone," *Time* magazine writes of fast-food restaurant massacres, homicide in small town America, and, quite dramatically, of "murder in the mall."[23]

It is this last article that to me is the most interesting, for it seems to point to the line of demarcation between what America regards as an acceptable level of violence and what is not. One of the stories in the article recounts the grisly strangulation of an 82-year-old retired schoolteacher who was murdered in her home in the small town of Tomball, Texas. One particular quote, that of the chief of police in Tomball, stands out. *Time* quotes him as saying of the murder, "This is a wake-up call for anyone in Tomball who may have got complacent about living here. Nowhere is safe." Nowhere indeed. Suburbia can no longer count itself immune from the dangers of violent crime. Who would have thought that a parent would be afraid to send his or her child to school? Who would have dreamed that the highway robbers of a bygone era would return to rob and to kill in the 1990s? The violence has spilled over into the safe zones. The demilitarized zones are no more.

And so we have mobilized our forces once again, it would seem. The war on crime is begun anew. The voice of the public has clamored for action, and action it shall have. So say the politicians. But how much ground will be taken in the battles ahead? How much more committed to victory are we today? Will we press onward without pause until the enemy is vanquished, or will the campaign hold fast upon its approach to the established parallel?

I see no reason to expect that we will drive across the old frontiers to liberate our country's most pitiable victims of crime. It is, after all, because we have failed to carry the battle to the enemy in campaigns past that we are compelled to wage the fight anew. It is the price we pay for reliance upon half measures instead of accepting the need to pursue more difficult but more efficacious solutions to our problems. There is no panacea. There is no magic formula for peace.

So long as we are satisfied with holding violence to an "acceptable level" as the solution to the problem of crime in America, the potential for a larger conflagration will always lurk beneath the surface. So long as there are places in our cities where children must sleep in bathtubs so as to be protected from stray gunfire, our suburbs and rural districts run the risk of renewed attacks. Should we chase the enemy back across the no-man's-land and merely reestablish the safety zones that we have traditionally held, we will only guarantee that violent crime will return to fight another day. Sadly, perhaps our greatest hope that we might at last be committed to an all-out campaign against crime is due to the heightened threat of an escalating conflict. The long-term trend of violence has reached an all-time high. Americans are dying at a rate more than five times what it was at the beginning of the twentieth century, and more are being killed by their fellow citizens than ever have been as far back as our records can reasonably carry us. Perhaps fear will finally motivate us to act.

NOTES

1. John Conroy, *Belfast Diary* (Boston, 1987), 5.
2. Ibid.
3. Ibid., 38.
4. Ibid., 39.
5. Ibid., 85.
6. Ibid., 39.
7. *Uniform Crime Reports* (Washington, DC, 1991), 15.
8. Ibid.
9. Ibid.
10. Ted Robert Gurr, "Historical Trends in Violent Crime: A Critical Review of the Evidence," in *Violence and Theft*, ed. Eric H. Monkkonen (New York, 1992), 444 447.
11. Ibid., 444.
12. Ibid.
13. Ibid.
14. *Uniform Crime Reports*, 1991.
15. *Report to the Nation on Crime and Justice* (Washington, DC, 1988), 15 and *Uniform Crime Reports*, 1991.
16. Keith D. Harries, *Serious Violence: Patterns of Homicide and Assault in America* (Springfield, IL, 1990), 12-18.
17. Jeffrey H. Reiman, *The Rich Get Richer and the Poor Get Prison* (New York, 1979), 16.
18. Ibid.
19. Ibid.
20. Ibid., 46-53.
21. *Time*, August 2, 1993, 22.

22. "Violence in the Schools," *U.S. News & World Report*, November 8, 1993, 34.

23. *Time*, August 23, 1993, 29-31.

11

A War of Many Fronts

To state that I have attacked the status quo in the field of law enforcement is to put the point mildly. Without question this essay constitutes a vociferous assault upon the actions, as well as the motivations, of a great number of the politicians and administrators who are responsible for criminal justice policy and its implementation. It also admonishes those professionals, no matter their rank, who bend their will to the corrupting influences of political hacks and power wielding-elites who seek to subordinate the administration of justice to their own ends. And it is hoped that through the vehicle of the polemic, a certain level of insight into the importance of ethical decision making might serve to inform those possessing a good heart—and there are many in policework–that they can make a difference in their chosen field of endeavor. They need only ask a simple question: Why?

It is possible, after all, to make what amounts to an ethical error. So long as one believes in the stated goals of the organization and buys into its public strategy for achieving them, one might devote a lifetime of effort to the cause of public safety without ever realizing that one has, in truth, served the ends of a second and less noble agenda. The error that may have been committed in such a scenario is one of simple omission: the failure to investigate just why campaigns such as the war against drugs continue to be waged again and again without so much as a modest advance on the field. It is one in which the police officer or administrator fails to ask why, in a so-called war to save society as we know it, the vast majority of casualties suffered are taken by the innocent civilians he or she is sworn to protect.[1] It takes a stout heart to fight against a system so large, and it takes a determined mind to question the assertions of agency chiefs and their command staffs. It calls for professional courage, indeed, for a police administrator to confront the political trends of the day and to call into question the policies of a mayor or a county executive. It is far easier to throw up one's hands and shake one's head while uttering the all too familiar refrain, "There's nothing I can do about it."

For far too many the job of policing has become just that—a job. I cannot begin to count the number of times that I and others I have worked with have simply shrugged our shoulders and resigned ourselves to merely putting in our time and collecting our paychecks. The bureaucratic politics of policing are like a well-worn record in law enforcement circles. Everybody knows the tune. If you want to get ahead, you have to know the right people, and if you want to demonstrate initiative, you have to write a lot of tickets. Almost as if in testimony to a failure to achieve, there are officers whose chests are adorned with ribbons that were issued for writing the most citations in their squad. Flash and revenue collection have won out in the field of policework. Looking good on paper has become the plan of action. Statistics gathering has come to rival bravery and diligent service as deserving of the highest honors.

Such a condition cannot be permitted to continue if we are to be effective in reducing the violence and degradation that assail our population every day. Body counts are hard to ignore, and the retreat of civilization before the onslaught of urban warfare is a frightening alternative to the remobilization of law enforcement and other assets at our disposal. America must reasses the threat it faces by availing itself of the wealth of useful intelligence at its disposal. New and more efficacious fronts must be opened on the battlefield of the war on crime and drugs. Indeed, whole new theaters of battle must be opened up.

Let us look out from inside our bunker and determine where our best chances lie. We should be able to achieve a victory, considering that other nations and other periods have done so. There is no reason that America's citizens should be dying at the hands of their compatriots at a rate five or six times what it was at the turn of the twentieth century. There is no justification for allowing the people of our cities to live in a siege mentality when around the civilized world urban communities are living in peace. In the paragraphs that follow, we will look for a battle plan that just might succeed.

THE FRONT

There are many fronts upon which to engage the enemy in the war on crime—but who is the enemy? Is it the impoverished residents of an urban ghetto? No more so, I think, than were the impoverished residents of the hamlets of South Vietnam. Just as we learned, only after one of the longest military struggles of our history and after we had forfeited 50,000 lives, that killing peasants is to no avail when they defend no military objective, so we may yet come to understand that the many recruits of the gangs that occupy our inner cities do not command the higher ground. True, they pull the triggers of the guns that fell our citizens and officers alike, but they are mere pawns, as is every foot soldier in every war that has ever been fought or is likely to be. This is not to excuse or to play down the heinous nature of a wanton murder, nor is it to deny the culpability of the perpetrators of such acts. Rather, it is to point out the classic error that is in play. To focus only on the street battles and random violence of the fight for turf and drug market share being waged by street gangs without probing to determine the larger nature of the enemy that confronts us, is no less foolish than for a military commander to charge his troops across the forward lines of an opposing army without having considered what manner of weapons and strength of numbers might lie in the distance. The Pyrrhic defeat of which Jeffrey Reiman warned most surely awaits us on the other side if we continue to persist in the senseless policies of the recent past.[2]

Just as the most critical military objectives often lie well behind the front, so do the most important targets for the agencies of drug enforcement. They are the cartel strongholds of Bolivia, Colombia, and Peru. They are the traffickers who smuggle cocaine across our borders and the entrepreneurs who finance its purchase and distribution-many of whom hold positions of wealth and influence inside our own country. It is the unholy alliance between organized crime and those in law enforcement who have sold their souls for money and pleasure. It is the politics of power and the trendiness of fashionable thinking. To engage the enemy, we must first identify who they are; and they do not look at us only from behind the eyes of an uncivilized youth. As often as not, they walk among us. As likely as not, they wear a uniform or a suit. To fight them, we must be willing to expose them. To win, we must be willing to destroy them.

THE ENEMY WITHIN

Veteran officers know who the enemies within are. They speak of their misdeeds among themselves and within the familiar confines of a squad car or a trusted companion's backyard. They are the cop who has been seduced by the easy lifestyle of one who is "friendly" with those known to have the wrong connections. They are the commander whose soul was long ago purchased for the price of a good deal on a new car or an easier rise up the promotional ladder. Rarely are they ever exposed for what they are, and seemingly they are immune to the law and to the discipline of the department. They are not all necessarily corrupted in the sense that cash bribes are taken or that criminal statutes have been violated ,but often they are culpable in another sense.

Membership in the elite circles of the quasi-legitimate players in the drug trade, even mere familiarity with the more fashionable side of the criminal element, has a way of blurring the judgment and blunting the resolve of both the police executive and the street-level officer. The contention that crime does not pay fails to take into account the roughly 90 percent of the criminals who never get caught and the more successful of them who live quite fabulously on their ill-gotten gains. Many have respected lives as business leaders and professionals of every stripe, and theirs is a bizarre and shadowy existence indeed. In her ethnography of drug smugglers and high-level distributors of cocaine, marijuana, and other drugs, Patricia Adler writes of the lifestyle or "flash" of such people.

Dealers and smugglers plunged themselves fully into satisfying their immediate desires whether these involved consuming lavish, expensive dinners, drugging themselves to saturation, traveling hundreds of miles to buy a particular item that caught their eye, or "crashing" (sleeping) for 15-20 hours at a time to make up for nights spent in unending drug use.[3]

Adler explains that those who live the fast life of the high-rolling, drug trafficking subculture are not constrained by the mundane requirements of everyday living. They revel in the intoxicating amounts of cash that the drug trade brings them and live hedonistic lives of excess in travel, sex, and consumption of every sort.

At the same time, the entrepreneurial criminals whom Patricia Adler studied live most of their lives outside of jail and among the population, plying their trade with impunity. For them, the police are but a minor irritation. She writes:

This confidence rested partly on their belief that police and drug agents were basically stupid and/or inept. Dealers pictured law enforcement as an administrative jungle, a morass of loosely connected police agencies who were constantly involved in competitive in-fighting. According to their perceptions, the specific agents who worked on drug busts were usually low on the enforcement status hierarchy, such as local narcs whom they thought made sloppy or illegal arrests frequently. Dealers and smugglers held some agencies in high esteem and feared them (the FBI and IRS), but according to subcultural lore, members of these agencies were not often assigned to drug work. They thus believed that the main task of catching them was left to the lower-echelon drug task forces and the unspecialized local patrols.[4]

The above quotation ought to have a ring of familiarity for the reader. Indeed, these cocaine-snorting, marijuana-smoking drug traffickers seem to have scored a bullseye on several points. Certainly, both our A-MEG example and the examination of the contradictory reports on the federal strike forces turned up similar conclusions. There is something structurally unsound about throwing together a potpourri of enforcement agencies under a less than fully empowered commander and commissioning such an entity to win the war on drugs.   It results in factionalism and inefficiency, and the enemy has recognized this weakness. As to the belief that is held by these criminals that narcotics enforcement is a low priority, this has already been established by our examination of the budgets involved.   Certainly, their contention that the higher levels of law enforcement rarely become involved in drug investigations is correct. There are field offices of the FBI, for example, operating in regions with populations in the hundreds of thousands who could not muster sufficient personnel to handle a good bar fight at any given time, much less dismantle a large-scale cocaine ring. They are vastly understaffed for the task.

More to the point at the moment, however, is Adler's discussion of "monopolistic markets" in the drug trade.[5] They are those of the traditional organized crime families.   Adler explains how such organizations operate: "First, large syndicates such as the Mafia which seek to dominate a market monopolistically generally develop connections with law enforcement agents. Syndicates use police to protect their members and operations, while driving their competitors out of business."[6]

Whenever the lid is blown off an arrangement such as this, it makes headlines, as any citizen of Miami or New York City will certainly be able to confirm. But the less formal world of the independent entrepreneur that Patricia Adler reveals to us in her study is, in a way, more insidious.

When one first confronts the idea that it is the "little" mistakes that sometimes have the biggest consequences, it is as though a darkened room has suddenly been flooded with light. Many an officer has stood in wonder at the incredible resilience of the criminal world. It is a tired and familiar comment that the idealistic rookie, over the course his or her career, will most often become just another cynic with a badge. Unable to comprehend the cause of the failure and uncertain whether it makes sense anymore to ask why, the typical officer will come to conclude that there is nothing he or she can do but try to hold the line where it is. It is a realization that attacks the will and dims the resolve of the police. Patrol officers and chiefs alike resign themselves to the status quo. I have been there. But pattern emerges if one looks past the surface. The status quo exists for a reason. It is the set point of civilization, to borrow a term from the medical arts.[7] It is where we have chosen to be. Whether one subscribes to the theories of Reiman, or of Stojkovic and Lovell, or finds a more sinister cause for the malady, it is best to understand that there are limits to what any given society is willing to achieve.

So it is with professions, fraternities, communities, and any group, and it allows for those on the fringe. There are always those who are willing to rationalize away the unethical nature of the free set of golf clubs or the fancy "samples" of the latest police equipment. It is a minor thing in their eyes, but it is the beginning of a complicity that will serve to disarm their agencies and departments. What is the harm of buying into the football pool at the local tavern? What can it hurt to play the ponies, just a little? Only their honor, I would answer, and with it their ability to perform their duty. Little wonder that raids on sports betting rings so rarely end in harsh prison sentences and numerous convictions. Little wonder, indeed, that they so rarely occur. And why should it be surprising that certain wealthy but ill-reputed members of the community seek to attach themselves to prominent police officials?

Time and again the rookie will ask himself or herself why the police can never seem to get to the kingpins. The officers will pound their desks in frustration and eventually give up, by and large. Yet it might be that the answer is not so complicated but merely a little too obvious to notice. The police do not focus most of their resources on the large-scale traffickers, and rarely do they seek to engage the wealthy businessmen who broker and finance the biggest deals of all. It might be that the reason for this is just what the criminology student of whom I spoke in an earlier chapter concluded—the kingpins are too difficult to outwit. I submit to the reader, however, that far too often, law enforcement has simply compromised itself.

TRENDINESS AND FASHIONABLE THINKING

Proactive patrol, selective incapacitation, cannabis enforcement and suppression effort, intensive sanctions, community policing, diversion, mandatory sentencing, community-based corrections, decriminalization, truth in sentencing, highway interdiction, demand-side enforcement, the war on crime, the war on drugs—each is a fad that has had its day, and each has served many masters. Driven by ideology and the need to promote the vested interests of the myriad stakeholders within the arena of politics and criminal justice, they are, in terms of substance, meaningless. Truly, the complexity of the criminal justice problem is such that issues like the etiology of crime and the impact of drug addiction on criminal behavior may never be completely understood. Because of this, there is much room for the purveyors of scientific snake oil to sell their wares to an unsuspecting public. Proponents of the various programs that are engineered as solutions to such problems as recidivism and crime prevention are so diverse in their political philosophies and theoretical schools as to cause the head to reel.

Still, the public demands that there be answers, and politicians have mandated that they be found—and found they have been. Bureaucrats and academics, professional consultants and political activists, government commissions and high-powered think tanks have all been analyzing data and constructing better programs for the alleviation of crime. Each of the many camps that have sprung up around this industry has a particular theory to espouse and a specific agenda to promote. Most of them have budgets, jobs, and political turf to protect. And whether one is trying to deflect attention away from the failure of law enforcement and its allies or pursuing failure as a means of promoting a political agenda of scapegoating the poor, nothing will achieve the goal better than the latest and most fashionable pseudoscientific technique for reducing crime.

Criminological research, just as any other body of scientific knowledge, can serve ideological or bureaucratic ends just as readily as it can serve the advancement of positive social goals. Indeed, this is the entire point of Jeffrey Reiman's Pyrrhic defeat theory. By selectively collecting and analyzing some data while ignoring others, one can frequently arrive at whatever conclusion will support the practitioner's or researcher's favorite theory. At the very heart of Reiman's assessment of the American system of justice is the contention that the police focus on street crime while ignoring white-collar and corporate crime.[8] He notes, for example, that while 9,285 members of the work force lost their lives due to crime in 1972, 100,000 of them died as the result of occupational hazards.[9] It is Reiman's contention that many of the latter deaths were preventable, and thus were tantamount to negligent homicides. It is no wonder, then, he contends, that corporate interests use their influence to ensure that no legislation that would make such negligence prosecutable comes into being while, at the same time, supporting the aggressive pursuit of street gangs, burglars, and robbery suspects.

Samuel Walker does an excellent job of illustrating the impact of ideology on criminology and the American system of justice. In his book *Sense and Nonsense About Crime and Drugs*, he describes what he refers to as the conservative theology[10] and the liberal theology[11] of crime control:

Conservative crime control theology envisions a world of discipline and self-control; people exercise self-restraint and subordinate their personal passions to the common good. It is a place of limits and clear rules about human behavior. The problem with criminals is that they lack self-control.[12]

So goes Walker's account of the stance of the right. He goes on to assess the position of the left on issues of crime as well:

Liberal crime control theology views the world as a large and idealized school. It explains criminal behavior in terms of social influences. People do wrong because of bad influences in the family, the peer group, or the neighborhood, or because of broader social factors, such as discrimination and lack of economic opportunity.

The liberals' solution to crime is to create a different set of influences. Rehabilitation involves shaping the offender in the direction of correct behavior.[13]

Having set the stage, Walker goes on to explain that each of these camps has set upon a quest for its own brand of success. He describes the liberal push for reforms in the area of corrections as "the story of a continuing search for the Holy Grail of rehabilitation."[14] As for the conservative tendency to equate deterrence with parental discipline, he tells us that "The real world, unfortunately, does not work like family discipline."[15] Walker then supports these characterizations of the liberal and conservative schools of criminology by debunking several of the programs the two sides support and the claimed successes for each.

One example used by Walker is that of the mandatory sentencing programs so near and dear to the hearts of law-and-order conservatives. The state of New York's 1973 drug law mandating lengthy prison terms is one of those examined. The law provided that convicted heroin dealers would serve minimum, mandatory prison terms ranging from one year to life for minor offenders, and fifteen years to life for major offenders (those who either sold an ounce of heroin or possessed two ounces of the substance). It was found, however, that between 1972 and 1976, "the overall percentage of arrests leading to conviction fell from 33.5 to 20 percent."[16] Walker points out that members of the "courtroom work group"[17] (prosecutors, judges, and defense attorneys) were able to evade the intent of the law by selectively charging and dismissing the offenders. Although he concedes that there was some modest success, in that the rate of incarceration did go up for those who were convicted, the effect of the law was essentially nullified.[18]

The claim that mandatory sentencing programs are, by and large, not successful is further supported by the experiences of both the state of Florida and the federal system. Even though Florida passed mandatory sentencing laws in 1975 and 1988, no significant impact on sentencing practices has resulted. Walker again points out that such factors as judicial discretion and "good time" reduction of prison terms effectively negated the laws' impact as an effective tool for reducing crime.[19] The story for the federal system is similar, though it must be conceded that the length of prison terms for those convicted did increase. Walker points out that this served to greatly increase the prison population and add to overcrowding. At the same time, however, correctional officials employed a greater use of "good time" programs in an effort to ease these conditions. The result is that whatever benefit might have been realized has again been negated.[20]

An example of how Samuel Walker explains the failure of the left to come up with the right answers to the question of how to control crime is found in his account of the Martinson Report. This 1974 criminological report by Robert Martinson resulted from a review of all of the evaluations of correctional programs that were available in English-language publications between 1945 and 1967. Walker informs us that most of this universe of data was eliminated as not being scientifically valid, for the Martinson team found that they were lacking such vital research components as control groups or drew "questionable conclusions from the data."[21] The upshot of the study was that although Martinson did find some positive results from correctional rehabilitation, he also stated that "with few and isolated exceptions, the rehabilitative efforts that have been reported so far have had no appreciable effect on rehabilitation."[22] Follow-up studies of the type conducted by Martinson, Walker indicates, have resulted in similar findings, fueling a long-term debate on the efficacy of rehabilitation programs.

Samuel Walker makes it clear that practitioners and researchers alike are guilty of wishful thinking and of stacking the deck in favor of their individual arguments. Time and again he demonstrates that many of the so-called successes in rehabilitation have been invented rather than achieved. Closer attention to ethical decision making might have served to advance the state of criminology in these instances, just as it might aid in achieving a more effectively run police department. A brief look at two of Walker's examples will be illustrative.

Diversion is one of the programs Walker examines, and he chooses the Manhattan Court Employment Project as an example.[23] In this program employment services were provided to underemployed and unemployed defendants–not facing homicide, rape, kidnapping, or arson charges.[24] Such persons were granted a delay of prosecution and could have their cases dismissed if they secured stable employment. A program evaluation conducted shortly after the project was initiated gave it high marks, including a 48.2 percent success rate and a very low cost. Later, however, another study found that recidivism was not abated and that the cost figures were misleading. Walker explains that this was due to the "net-widening syndrome,"[25] a situation in which low risk offenders who would otherwise have their cases dismissed were selected for inclusion in the diversion program. The result, of course, is a skewing of statistics and the incurring of a cost that would otherwise not have been necessary. "The net-widening phenomenon suggests that the 'old' diversion did a better job," writes Walker.[26] Walker notes that what he means by this is that district attorneys who declined to prosecute and police officers who elected not to arrest offenders for minor violations of the law did a far more cost-effective and less intrusive job of diversion than did the Manhattan Court Employment Project.

Walker also takes a look at intensive probation supervision (IPS), another of the many fads to hit the rehabilitation scene. In IPS programs, probationers are closely supervised with a great number of contacts between the client and the probation officer, frequent testing of drugs, and generally much tighter restrictions on behavior and movements. Not all that surprisingly, Walker finds that such programs are not new. As evidence of this he cites the San Fransisco Project, an IPS program that was put into place during the 1960s.[27]

The San Fransisco Project, a federal program of intensive probation supervision, was subjected to systematic evaluation at the time. Control groups were set up, reports Walker, for the purpose of comparing the new intensive measures with more traditional and less restrictive ones. The evaluators learned that there was "no significant difference in the recidivism rates of

offenders in the various groups."[28]   Walker points out that there are similar
findings in studies of the newest wave of IPS programs. Evaluations recently
conducted in California, New Jersey, and Georgia are equally disheartening.
"IPS suffers from both confused goals and exaggerated promises," he writes.[29]

So what are we to make of all of this? Confusion and a seemingly endless
series of fits and starts appear to constitute our best effort at finding a solution
to crime and violence.   Jeffrey Reiman provides us with a very solid
explanation for this in chapter 4 of his book, *The Rich Get Richer and the Poor
Get Prison*.[30] As he goes about the task of explaining how the public is fooled
into thinking that the poor are the source of the most dangerous crimes,
Reiman turns to the concepts of ideology and propaganda. He writes:

In simple terms, because those who have economic power (i.e., those who have control
over the means of material production) own the newspapers, endow the universities,
finance the publications of books and journals, and (in our own time) control the
television and radio industries, they have a prevailing say in what is said, heard, and
thought by (i.e., they have control over the means of mental production for) the millions
who get their ideas–their picture of   reality–from these sources.[31]

Reiman asserts that worldviews are engineered, as it were, by the prevailing
power structures. Whether this is unconsciously achieved and accepted (the
form of ideology) or is accomplished with deliberate deception (propaganda),
ideals and beliefs are packaged and sold to the waiting public. The interests of
the elite are well served by this, for if the lower classes did not buy into the
prevailing political system, there would be dissention or worse.   Reiman
himself puts it best:

When I speak of ideology, I mean the conscious or unconscious use of ideas (or images
or other 'messages'), not for the purpose of conveying the truth, but falsely to justify (or
legitimate) the prevailing distribution of power and wealth and thus to secure allegiance
to (or undermine opposition to) the social order characterized by that distribution of
power and wealth.[32]

We can use this perspective to help inform us on two levels in the current
discussion, the political and the administrative. As Samuel Walker made clear,
the liberal vs conservative debate over the meaning of criminological research
and the proper solutions to the problem of crime has not served us well.
Ideological wars do not often bring about the most careful search for truth.
Ideology and propaganda, as Reiman tells us, "connote the use of ideas to
achieve a political goal instead of to achieve truth."[33] The truth, then, often
gets lost in the debate.

As we know from Matthew Holden's writing on bureaucratic politicians,
there is little difference between an agency administrator and an elected official
when it comes to making a grab for money. Realizing this is significant when

trying to understand what would otherwise only be viewed as quixotic behavior on the part of law enforcement agencies across the country. Grantsmanship and the quest for budget do more to determine how the police will do business today than any mission statement that might hang on the wall at the public safety building. It explains why C-City and the County created A-MEG within in a matter of weeks once federal monies became available for multijurisdictional task forces, though the two governments had failed to come to terms on such a unit for decades prior to such appropriations being made available.

It makes clear just why for every decade there is a new fad in law policing. In the 1970s the street cop was all the rage and investigators clad in casual civilian attire took the job to the intimate level of the fence and the junkie. With the 1980s came the wave of counter-drug task forces and specialized narcotics units, established to counter the threat posed by the newly arrived and more sophisticated kingpin. And in the 1990s we have once again risen to the occasion with the creation of the gang unit. Armed with the specialized expertise of the "gang crimes investigator," we have yet again succumbed to the latest fad in law enforcement circles. It begins to form a predictable pattern. It begins to have a familiar ring.

It does not matter how one wraps the package, the contents are always the same. A failed policy is a failed policy, no matter how one might couch its intention in euphemistic rhetoric or disguise its content with hardware and "flash." Until police administrators comprehend that the bulk of their crime-fighting resources are squandered on diversions they will continue to miss the point. So long as such executives regard revenue collection as a legitimate function of traffic patrol, they will be complicit in the perversion of the administration of justice. And to the extent that they continue to divert their personnel from targeting kingpins by insisting that they chase statistics instead, the chiefs of police and agents-in-charge who stand at the helm of the law enforcement effort in this country will continue to enable the most insidious of the criminals among us to prey upon the citizens for whom the law enforcement agencies are responsible.

Once again we see the error of omission in operation. The crime, again, is the failure to ask why. Why, a law enforcement executive might ask himself or ask herself, throughout the years, has every program that has been tried, failed to bring results? Why, such an administrator might wonder, does every battle waged in the war on crime yield nothing but a slightly higher body count and an even less promising future? Why, the chief might inquire, though we hurl wave after wave of troops against the front, do we never seem to capture the key objectives and the only prisoners we take are the lowly privates? Ask the questions enough times, and you will discover that they are the victims of the most insidious of betrayals—self-deception.

One owes a duty not only to others but to oneself when standing in a position of power and influence. A police administrator can be likened to a lottery winner. Everybody wants to be his or her best friend, and each of them wants his or her way. Some will flatter, others will buy, and many will gain influence through familiarity or favors. Politicians will wield their power either to the advantage of the administrator who sees the "wisdom" of going along or to the detriment of those who dare to assert their independence. The wealthy will bluster about crime in the street and, sadly, many who suffer from this malady that plagues us will side with them, taken in by the same rhetoric that has captured the police. One should consider the dangers of fashionable thinking and remember that it is wise to oppose that which makes no sense.

It should be remembered that, in the final analysis, it is the practitioner who must decide what must be done in the day-to-day operations of a police department or an enforcement bureau. Programs and innovations are all well and good, but philosophies of operation are important, too. I do not mean to revisit the well-worn debate of order maintenance vs. law enforcement by pointing this out, but I do intend to indicate that there is more to police administration than operational techniques or the implementation of the latest in prepackaged anti-crime programs. A police executive is more than a manager; he or she is a policymaker as well. As such, it is a mistake to lock one's focus on strategies and tactics while failing to use them to the best advantage. Far too often our chiefs and our sheriffs fail to address just what it is that they ultimately seek to achieve.

This failure to analyze the goals of the department reflects of the ideological trap that many administrators have fallen into. It is the reason why they continue to lock up drug abusers by the score while seeming to be unaware of the far greater threat presented by the brokers and traffickers of the enormous shipments of cocaine, heroin, and marijuana that continue to flood the black market. This state of affairs is more than quixotic-it is a rout from the attack. It is a failure by design. The drug lords are winning, and so are their allies living among us.

As evidence of this ideological defeat I would cite the obvious-the results compared with the rhetoric. From presidents to rookies of patrol we have heard the call to arms again and again. The "war on drugs," the "war on crime," "more cops on the street," go the political slogans. We have heard of the effort to overcome the drug lords and the smugglers via the television news and in magazines. Press releases regarding such law enforcement efforts as "Operation Green Merchant" and "Operation Snowcap" come and go along with the latest in fashions from New York. And, in the midst of all of this fire and maneuver, a rallying cry that is a simultaneous surrender issues forth. "We are losing," comes the cry. "We are losing the war and so we must fight on." It is a frightening realization to draw a lesson from this echo. It seems that just as we failed to see the fallacy of the colonial policies of the French in Vietnam, and so were drawn into the most hopeless of all of the conflicts in which we have fought, we have failed to realize the impiety of relegating the burden of our ideological battles to the American ghetto. And more to our chagrin is the fact that we have decided to suffer the same fate as did the French at the battle of Dien Bien Phu, thinking that somehow we can hold out against the odds if only we can drop more troops into the fray.34

It is the objectives that are flawed, not the tactics. If our object is to rack up arrests and convictions, then we are a resounding success. Our jails are full. We are building more prisons every day. Convicts stream through our institutions and patients wait in line for a thirty-day stint in drug rehabilitation centers. People are lying or at least they are fooling themselves. Just as the human waves of the Viet Minh forces overwhelmed the technology and the tactics of the French, so the waves of convicts and addicts will continue to defeat our best. Until the police learn that they are simply off the target, they will always miss the mark. Until the politicians realize that merely to spout rhetoric is to tell a vicious lie, they will continue to mislead us. So long as ideology succeeds in obfuscating reality, we will persist in fighting this senseless war against ourselves.

ORGANIZED CRIME AND THE CARTELS

Early in this book I mentioned the annual Red, Green, and White Books or reports issued from the White House under the title *National Drug Control Strategy*. One of the predecessors to this series is a report issued from the Office of the Attorney General, *Drug Trafficking: A Report to the President of the United States.*35 In this document one will find the various drug trafficking organizations that the attorney general had identified as being a threat to the American public. They include the following:

Colombian drug cartels
La Cosa Nostra and the Sicilian Mafia
Asian organized crime groups
Jamaican posses
Outlaw motorcycle gangs
California street gangs
Other domestic trafficking organizations
Trafficking by other foreign nationals.

The Colombian cartels are depicted in the report as being highly organized with a structure characterized by "an onion-like layering of organizational power, with kingpins at the center, directing operations but insulated by layer upon layer of protective subordinate operatives."36 Four principal cartels are cited; the Medellin' cartel, the Cali cartel, the Bogota' cartel, and the north

Atlantic coast cartel. They are portrayed as immensely wealthy, and it is noted that they are estimated to own one-twelfth of the farmland in Colombia.[37] They are seen as extremely violent and are skilled at employing intimidation and violence to counter law enforcement and resistance by legitimate business. The report describes them as having "a propensity for violence that has not been seen in the American underworld since the bootleg days of prohibition in the 1920's and early 1930's."[38]

The report also speaks of La Cosa Nostra (LCN) and the Sicilian Mafia. It informs us that there are about twenty-five families with thousands of members who do big business in drug trafficking. Of course, this is in addition to the traditionally identified enterprises of vice, gambling, and racketeering that are so infamously tied to these organizations. The document goes on to state that although the highest levels of LCN and Mafia leadership have been "devastated" by government inroads,[39] lower-level members have reorganized and still present a high-level threat.

The report drones on, ticking off the many dangerous organized criminal gangs that exist in America today. There are the outlaw motorcycle gangs who traffick in methamphetamine, marijuana, and PCP. There are the international gangs such as the Jamaican posses and others who have rushed in to exploit the market for drugs and the opportunities for racketeering that present themselves in our open society. It warns of the street gangs of California and the "traditional criminal organizations" of such cities as Chicago and Detroit.[40]

There is no doubt that America is confronted by numerous gangs and organized criminal enterprises. Whether one is given to relying on the government for this discovery in reports such a those churned out by presidential commissions[41] or would prefer to search it out in academic works such as Howard Abadinsky's, *The Mafia in America: An Oral History,*[42] the evidence is there. What needs to be stressed, however, is that such entities as the Cali cartel and the Mafia could not succeed to the extent that they do without the complicity of supposedly legitimate businesses and the corruption of public officials. They need banks in which to launder money and banking officials who will allow them to do so. They need real estate transactions to hide illicit profits and police departments and enforcement bureaus that find no need to search the records of such commerce. Such criminals rely upon an ideological, and morally flawed, stance in law enforcement that wages war against its own population while honoring an armistice with the most despicable of America's enemies. In this there is a need for change.

We can find a hope for a better understanding of this circumstance in the writing of Dwight C. Smith, Jr. In his "*Ideology and the Ethics of Economic Crime Control,*"[43] Smith writes of how ideology has polarized criminology in its view of economic crime. "Morally centered judgments reflect the ideology of the writer, with organized crime cast as a morally reprehensible creature in the eyes of the right, and white-collar crime as the more common focus of the left."[44] Smith reminds us of the rift between criminologists of the left and those of the right, and points out how each group attacks its favorite villain while taking the roles of a *moral entrepreneur*.[45] The right assails the Mafia and Cosa Nostra as corrupt and immoral machines bent on the destruction of legitimate government. The left depicts the corporate criminal as the primary antagonist in league with the mob. Indeed, traditional organized crime is viewed in this perspective as a servant of the corporate criminal and as a natural consequence of a capitalist society.

Smith attempts to reorder these perspectives in such a way as to note the fact that white-collar and business crime is properly positioned on a continuum along with traditional organized crime. As he puts it, "Behavior patterns that have traditionally defined one are increasingly recognized as present in the other."[46] They can be better understood as arrayed along an "entrepreneurial spectrum."[47] Each is engaged in economic crime. Each relies on corruption, organization, and human weakness to forward its own financial gain through extralegal enterprises. Moralizing needs, in this view, to be set aside, as does ideology.

Although Smith was writing primarily about the need for criminology to deal with ideology and moral bias in research and debate, there is a strong practical lesson to be learned from him. Ethical considerations as impacted by ideology are key in the decision-making processes that confront our law enforcement executives. A police administrator must take a stance on such matters that does not allow for the bigotry of ideologues to sway his or her judgment when it comes to the deployment of resources and the selection of policy for the agency under his or her leadership. It is morally incumbent upon such executives and managers to attack the problem of crime on all of its fronts—not just the popular ones. It is ethically necessary for the commander of an organized crime unit to go after the financier as well as the street boss. Organized crime is indeed a great threat to America today. The flood of drugs available to our youth and the corruption of official justice are grave indeed, not to mention an enormous drain on our economic resources. But to fight the war on crime only halfway is to lose the campaign. Indeed, America may already be mired in a modern-day Vietnam. For all of the caution we have invested in avoiding another senseless war abroad, we may have failed to prevent a massive invasion of our own sovereign soil.

NOTES

1. Samuel Walker, *Sense and Nonsense About Crime and Drugs* (Belmont, CA, 1994), 8.
2. Jeffrey H. Reiman, *The Rich Get Richer and the Poor Get Prison* (New York, 1979), 16-17.

3. Patricia A. Adler, *Wheeling and Dealing* (New York, 1985), 84.

4. Ibid., 109.

5. Ibid., 118-121.

6. Ibid., 119.

7. "Set point" is the term used in medical and nutritional circles to describe that body weight to which any given idividual tends to gravitate.

8. Reiman, *The Rich Get Richer*, 57-86.

9. Ibid., 66.

10. Walker, *Sense and Nonsense*, 17-19.

11. Ibid., 19-20.

12. Ibid., 17.

13. Ibid., 19.

14. Ibid.

15. Ibid., 18.

16. Ibid., 92.

17. Ibid., 48.

18. Ibid., 92.

19. Ibid., 87-88.

20. Ibid., 95.

21. Ibid., 209.

22. Ibid., 208-209.

23. Ibid., 212.

24. Ibid.

25. Ibid., 213.

26. Ibid., 214.

27. Ibid.

28. Ibid.

29. Ibid., 220.

30. Reiman, *The Rich Get Richer*, 138-169.

31. Ibid., 157.

32. Ibid., 159.

33. Ibid., 158.

34. Dien Bien Phu was a French air base on a low plain surrounded by mountains. It was believed by the generals of France to be invincible to assault by the Viet Minh who opposed them. They learned otherwise. Ho Chi Minh overcame logistical problems thought to have been insurmountable by his adversaries by employing sheer human effort in a trek across thousands of miles of difficult terrain and launched a massive atttack against the base. As the Viet Minh advanced toward their perimeter, the French parachuted in thousands of additional troops in a vain attempt to hold out. In the end, French officers were requesting permission to withdraw and escape but were ordered to hold with their troops to the last. The carnage was massive, and the air base fell to the Viet Minh.

35. *Drug Trafficking: A Report to the President of the United States* (Washington, DC, 1989).

36. Ibid., 17.

37. Ibid., 19.

38. Ibid., 20.

39. Ibid., 22.

40. Ibid., 33-38.

41.   E.g., President's Commission on Organized Crime, *The Impact: Organized Crime Today* (Washington, DC, 1986).

42. Howard Abadinsky, The Mafia in America: An Oral History (New York, 1981).

43.   Dwight C. Smith, Jr., "Ideology and the Ethics of Crime Control," in *Ethics, Public Policy, and Criminal Justice*, ed. Frederick Elliston and Norman Bowie (Cambridge, MA, 1982).

44. Ibid., 133.

45. Ibid., 134.

46. Ibid., 144.

47. Ibid.

12

The Reorganization

Policework is likely to change a great deal in the years ahead. President Clinton has called for an increase in the ranks of law enforcement personnel by a figure of 100,000 officers; many have been called for in the new 1994 crime bill. At the same time multijurisdictional drug task forces, or metropolitan enforcement groups, as they are also known, have lost federal funding under the present administration, and it remains to be seen whether they will survive. Across the country attempts are being made to reestablish the practice of foot patrol and to install community police units that will get neighborhood residents into the effort to combat street crime. Gang crime units are in operation throughout the country, and more are being established. Yet this state of rapid change or flux is nothing new. Indeed, it is a tired saw by now, for though policing races headlong into the future, it merely circles back upon itself.

A lack of innovation of technique is not the challenge policework must overcome if it is to make headway against crime. Rather, what is needed is a new sophistication in terms of selecting the goals of law enforcement. The programs that are listed in the paragraph above constitute the strategies and tactics of law enforcement as it sets about the business of waging the war on crime. They are the methods that have been selected for achieving a given end: crime reduction. The fact that these strategies and tactics have failed miserably, though they have been legion in number, should cause one to reexamine the objectives they pursue. The goal, after all, is crime reduction, a safer community; and certain objectives have been set in place to facilitate progress toward that end.

In the parallel example of achieving the goal of public health, a society will determine a set of objectives to be met in the overall effort designed to bring it about. Such objectives as the establishment of sanitary districts, hospitals and clinics, and a preschool inoculation program would be set. The strategies involved might be described as establishing visiting nurse associations, mobile clinics, and regionalized hospitals. Of course these could vary in that a given country or province might elect to put permanent clinics in place as opposed to mobile ones, or might choose to build neighborhood hospitals rather than regional institutions. As for tactics, these serve the given strategy in play and are even closer to the point of service, affecting such matters as how the clinics will be managed or how the mobile facilities will be financed. Each of these elements of the overall plan represents a different level of organization and purpose. Law enforcement, for some reason, seems never to have learned to distinguish between them properly.

The police and federal enforcement agencies seem consumed with method—with strategy and tactic—rather than with establishing goals and objectives. The administrators will, of course, defend this by informing us that it is the job of the political apparatus to determine law enforcement goals and the duty of the police to pursue them. This is true. The legislature is responsible for the passage of criminal statutes, and the executive is the entity that should provide a course of action for the officials who must enforce them. It is, however, also the job of the police to enforce the law in a just and impartial manner following the letter and the spirit of its meaning. There is no provision in the Constitution that instructs the police to enforce the law of the land selectively, in accordance with the prevailing ideology of the day. There is no mandate in the founding documents that compels the agencies that administer justice to bend the Constitution in response to the political will of the party that happens to hold the seat of power. The Constitution is the supreme law of the land, not a set of guidelines to consult for suggestions on how to go about the task of implementing government.

Law enforcement has far too often deferred to the prevailing ideology of the day, and it has done so by allowing ideology to select the objectives it will pursue rather than simply enforcing the laws as they have been written. It is the reason why narcotics raids almost invariably occur in the homes of low-level dealers and petty distributors of illegal drugs rather than in the mansions and towers of the entrepreneurs who finance and direct them. It is the reason why hundreds of thousands of the poor are locked up every year in the war on crime while white-collar criminals and millionaire money launderers are rarely incarcerated. It is a failure to devote resources where they will do the most good and a willingness, instead, to hunt down scapegoats marked for imprisonment by the powers that be. Just as the postarrest segment of the American criminal justice system meaninglessly pursues the quest for the "holy Grail of rehabilitation"[1] in the form of vacuous diversion programs and smoke-and-mirrors probation efforts, so the prearrest side defeats itself in a senseless game of cat and mouse.

Here we are once again confronted with the significance of character in the field of policework. Just which "bad guys" a police officer will decide to pursue is a matter of discretion. Judgment is required, and professional ethics comes into play in such situations. The same applies to law enforcement administrators, for as they go about the business of determining at what level to target criminals for arrest and harassment, they, too, exercise discretion. Police executives wield enormous power in this way, for it is they who decide whether to devote their personnel to the pursuit of high-level traffickers or of arresting street-level dealers. It is they who decide whether to emphasize the disruption of financial schemes to launder drug money or street-level stings designed to round up addicts and petty offenders.

Howard Cohen has written about the subject of police discretion in his essay titled "Authority: The Limits of Discretion."[2] In it he writes, "The use of discretion is not an option for police officers; it is a necessary, unavoidable part of their job."[3] He also makes clear, however, that such discretion is without formal authority. There is no statute or constitutional provision for police discretion. Officially, the law is simply to be enforced. The police are not to act as legislators or judges but are, according to the law, to detect crime and bring offenders before the courts for judgment. Cohen asserts that this is not possible to achieve, however, and that an officer who attempted to live out this standard "would either fail or stop working."[4] He is right, of course. The individual peace officer observes far more violations of the law than he or she could ever hope to process. To attempt to do so would be to become paralyzed and ineffective. The same applies to the police executive. There are, after all, far more demands for service and protection brought before a police chief or bureau head than can ever be met by the limited resources of a given enforcement agency.

Every police administrator, then, is faced with a set of dilemmas. Each of these executives must make choices about how he or she will expend limited personnel and equipment, just as each and every uniformed officer must decide how he or she will spend his or her limited time and energies on a given shift. How does one choose, the reader might ask? How should such an administrator go about determining how best to deploy the forces at his or her command? The answer is that police resources must be devoted in accordance with the objectives that have been selected to further the goals of the department or agency involved. They must also be prioritized with respect to their relative importance to those goals. Key to arriving at a solution to the problem of deciding what to do with the limited assets that are available, then, is the establishment of particular law enforcement objectives. Here again we are confronted with the need for discretion. Questions of ethics and morality are unavoidable.

Harold F. Gortner, Julianne Mahler, and Jeanne Bell Nicholson, in their book *Organization Theory*, refer to the existence of a "'culture' of government,"[5] and assert that one of the factors making up this culture can be described as "the values, mores, and habits of the primary actors, especially the elected and appointed officials and the bureaucrats working beneath those officials."[6] These authors contend that leadership operates within a culture defined by factors such as this along with others like "the history of government" and its role "as perceived by members of society."[7] They go on to point out that in large part, executive decision making consists of being aware of the importance of values and goals, and how they impact on different people and interests.[8] I agree. Bureau executives and chiefs of police function within a particular culture and are confronted with an established system of beliefs, promulgated alongside of, and often influenced by either a single, dominant ideology or competing ideologies vying for control of the machinery of justice. Not to realize this is to be administratively adrift.

Within the executive ranks of law enforcement there are decision makers of every stripe. Some buy into the stated agenda and strive throughout their careers to defeat the criminal element in all the wrong ways. These are the "good soldiers" of the law enforcement world. Armed with the latest enforcement program or the most sophisticated technology, they set out to capture the criminals who plague our communities. Others are more like the bulk of the rank and file. Cynical and aware, they "play the game" and, among themselves, will confess this. If it is statistics that will please the powers that be, it is statistics they will provide. If revenue is near and dear to the mayor or the county board, then they will see to it that the radar units are kept humming night and day. These are the commanders who have lost any hope of winning the battle, and they are perhaps best described as the "vanquished." But then there are those who both comprehend the true nature of the threat that confronts them and yet have not lost heart. These are indeed the remaining "knights of the realm." They are a rarity to be admired, for theirs is a lonely task and a difficult one.

The knights of the realm are the people's best hope in the campaign to bring "domestic tranquillity" to America's cities and towns. They are the reason that once in a very great while a corrupt politician will fall to the sword of official justice. They are the force behind the occasional breakup of a crime ring at the highest levels of organized crime. They know their objective and understand why certain risks must be taken if they are to win the day. And, even more to their credit, they are willing to suffer the consequences of their actions in the field.

DEFEATING THE ENEMY WITHIN

It is obvious by now that one of the primary objectives in a successful prosecution of the war on crime is the routing of the enemy among us. To date the effort has not been a credible one. Many police agencies of considerable size do not yet have an office of internal affairs within their organization and, sadly, not all of them that do, are using them as they should be. A personal story will serve to illustrate.

I have had one brush with an internal affairs officer; it involved nothing more than a scratched fender. I had the bad luck to scratch the fender of a squad car as I was in the process of parallel parking. I misjudged the distance between the squad car and another car already parked at the curb. A scuff on the outside corner of the bumper of the other car and a scratch to the paint of the right rear fender of the squad car were the results. As is appropriate, I went to the phone and contacted a supervisor, and a patrol car was dispatched to write up a report. Weeks passed, and nothing was made of the incident by my lieutenant. One day, however, an internal affairs officer came to my office to tell me that he was formally recommending that I be subjected to disciplinary action for "failure to maintain proper lookout." I was further informed that he had taken the matter up with the appropriate committee, and paperwork would issue shortly.

The IA man was correct. I had failed to see to it that the distance between my squad car and the civilian vehicle to its rear was sufficient to allow me to park. I deserved a ticket. However, no one intended to issue me a ticket because this was considered an internal matter. Internal disciplinary procedures were determined to be the correct course. I subsequently learned that such processing of actions against officers was not unique. Indeed, IA was quite busy with them and was responsible for all such personnel actions.

Little wonder that one rarely sees the regulations concerning such matters as consorting with felons applied to those police officers who think so little of their badge and oath that they will golf with known drug traffickers and dine with convicted felons. It seems remarkable, indeed, that throughout my career in drug enforcement I became aware of a number of reports that peace officers were involved in drug use and even drug sales, yet I can count the number of headlines concerning the arrest of such persons on the fingers of one hand. Internal affairs offices are far too busy with personnel matters instead.

It would seem that what is needed is an outside source of intervention if the criminal justice system is to come to grips with the problem of police corruption. One such outside agency could exist under the auspices of the office of the district attorney. Among the handful of successful police corruption cases that I have read about in the newspapers of my home state are those of the Milwaukee County district attorney's White Collar and Organized Crime Unit. Its investigators, employees of the district attorney, are not subject to the oversight of the police departments within their area of operation. The staff is devoted to uncovering both government corruption and white-collar crime, and they report to a prosecutor instead of a chief. Such agencies are a necessity in the future if we are to make genuine headway against corruption.

Another set of agencies more traditionally responsible for the policing of the police are the various state police units that have been charged with investigating official corruption. Unfortunately, the staffs of such units are often quite small, and many state police agencies are low-paying and considered to be at the entry level job the mainstream of law enforcement. This, I suspect, is the result of an overemphasis on the form of federalism that seeks to bypass the states and co-opt the cities. A lesson might well be taken from Jeffrey L. Pressman and Aaron Wildavsky's classic work, *Implementation*.[9] In this instance there is a need to upgrade the potential of many of the state police services that exist around the country. It has become obvious that the local police are not effective in investigating the ranks of their own, and as it stands, the states are ill-equipped to respond to the need. Standards of pay and education for state enforcement agents should be upgraded, and the staff should be increased substantially.

Of course, the Federal Bureau of Investigation has long held a responsibility for the investigation of police wrongdoing, but the reality has fallen short here as well. Understaffed, and with far too many areas of concern for a single agency, the FBI has not proved to be the solution to police corruption. The more candid of their agents will admit to the "locals," as they refer to the municipal and county police, that unless it involves a command staff officer or a serious felony, it is of little interest to them. Perhaps this is best. To require too many matters to cross the emperor's desk has never been wise. This serves to amplify the need to increase such resources at the state and county level, however.

THE BATTLE WITH THE IDEOLOGUES

Next there is the battle with the modern-day shamans who have laid claim to the status of "expert" in the fields of criminal justice and criminology. Here there is the need for a healthy dose of skepticism, for to be drawn into an endless parade of programs is to be distracted from the job of functioning as an executive should. First, the agency head should select the objectives to be pursued in light of the goals that have been set by the legislature and the executive. Only after this has been accomplished will there be time to listen to the din of proposals that are forever at the door. Here, there is a genuine need for professionalization and the expertise and standards it would bring to the police services.

Law enforcement has long been confused about the various aspects of its role and makeup. Particularly, it has suffered from an inability to come to grips with its own identity as either a profession or an occupation. Many have come to refer to it as a paraprofession, as in the example of a paralegal. In the 1970s there was the push to elevate the education of individual police officers by paying for a college degree, and many an officer received a Bachelor of Arts in criminal justice at federal expense. More and more, police academy requirements have been raised and minimum numbers of college credits are required for hiring by some of the bureaus of the various states. Yet there is something decidedly wrong with this process, for it mismatches the level of training and education with the positions that are held.

There are many applicants for the job of police officer who have four-year degrees and even graduate educations. At the same time there are many who do not have such credentials. Also, a large number who hold the rank of lieutenant or captain-and even chief-have no degree of any kind. Here we have yet another example of trendiness and fashionable thinking at work. In the 1960s there was a push for educating as many of our citizens at the college level as would care to take up the challenge. The LEAA was one of the mechanisms by which this could be achieved-at least it was for working police officers. Such degree candidates would have their tuition paid and criminal justice programs boomed. Upon the demise of the LEAA, many departments made use of tuition reimbursement programs and hiring bonuses to continue the flow of college-trained personnel. This was all well and good, but promotional practices lagged behind. After all, police administrators want lieutenants and captains they are comfortable with and not necessarily because they hold university degrees. Then, too, there were union contracts to contend with, and promotional practices that required a minimum standard of a college degree did not sit well with the police benevolent associations.

What has resulted is an ill-conceived and poorly constructed staffing situation. There are captains who have no idea of the intricacies of budget or personnel deployment and who are in no way prepared to function as consumers of research. It is no wonder that so much in the way of scientific snake oil ends up on the shelf at the local police department when the individual responsible for its purchase cannot tell the difference between medicine and poison. In order for such administrators to make judgments about policy and program issues for their department or bureau, there is a definite need for a functional appreciation for such tools as basic research statistics and program evaluation. It is therefore important that people responsible for the budgeting of millions of dollars of taxpayer monies be able identify the term "policy analysis" as something other than an insurance company marketing tool.

Conversely, the patrol officer and criminal investigator need highly technical knowledge and skills if they are to do their job well. Criminalistics, procedural and criminal law, firearms, and emergency medical procedures are a sampling of the course of study that is necessary if one is to become competent as a front lineofficer. Such personnel must be skilled at evidence collection and preservation, and must be cognizant of the pitfalls of sloppy procedure when responding to a report of a crime. Their report writing skills must be honed to a high level, and they must be capable of surviving a life-threatening confrontation with a criminal bent on escape. These are the technicians or paraprofessionals of law enforcement.

I would call for the establishment of a two-tier system of personnel in the field of policework, an idea that is not new but is certainly anything but prevalent. Executives and managers should be distinct from the ranks of the staff in the field, and the standards set for each must be tailored to the job at hand. Two-year technical degrees in police science of the type that provide the curriculum discussed above should be required for hiring at the entry level of policework. The skills so obtained are ideal for patrol and investigations; should more education be desired for the purpose of advancement, it can always be pursued. Managers such as lieutenants and captains should hold no less than a bachelor's degree upon being installed in such positions. To have less than this level of education is to be ill-prepared for such matters as personnel administration and statistical reporting. As for executive positions in law enforcement, there should be a requirement for a professional degree. A master's-level education in a discipline such as public administration or criminal justice should be demanded by the government body seeking to employ a new chief, sheriff, or bureau executive. Such a level of administration requires no less than professional judgment, and in view of the salaries commanded by such persons, no less than professional competence should be required.

Rather than simply mimic the military system with its officer corps and enlisted ranks, the police should genuinely employ it in an effort to arrive at a truly professionalized status. The officer corps of the military services exists because it provides a tangible means for ensuring the highest qualities of leadership and organization possible. Just as the words "officer and gentleman" connote professionalism and ethics in the military, so they should evoke the same form of conduct and character within the ranks of the police. It is vital that those who hold command positions in law enforcement quit talking about professionalization and go about the business of implementing it. Of course, elected officials must lead the way, but they are less likely to do so if their police executives are blocking the way.

Once a truly professional cadre of police administrators is in place, they can begin to select the objectives of their respective departments or bureaus. Many of these should already be forming in the reader's mind. Keeping the goal in mind, the objectives will quickly materialize. If the disruption of drug trafficking is the goal, then the objectives are simple to list. At the federal level they entail border interdiction and the investigation of money laundering schemes. Such objectives call for increased border surveillance, and so an increase of personnel and equipment is necessary. They require accountants and agents operating in foreign countries who seek to uncover the illegal transfer and concealment of funds. We need more of them. State-level objectives might include the disruption of local distribution rings and the detection of money laundering schemes. The obvious need for intelligence gathering and specialized expertise should cause the director of a state bureau of investigation to push for more highly trained agents and for the most sophisticated intelligence mechanism that can be made available. Federal promises of a new mulitjurisdictional task force (translation: A-MEG) is no replacement for genuine assets. The latest fad should be seen for what it is and the director should find the political and moral courage to resist the easier path of going along.

A sheriff or police chief must use similar judgment when selecting a set of objectives for his or her department. He or she should resist the temptation to chase street gangs and petty offenders while ignoring the "pillar of society" who goes about the business of brokering the shipments of drugs with impunity. A new and more intense focus should be placed on detecting hidden assets and on the technical skills to search real estate records for "land flips" (real property transactions designed to bury drug profits in legitimate commerce) and to analyze incoming intelligence in a truly sophisticated way. Little is accomplished by purchasing a costly and powerful software application designed to ferret out cocaine rings if it is used so ineptly that it is little more than a filing system.

White-collar crime and organized crime units should be installed within the offices of state and county prosecutors. These should be staffed with independent investigators under the authority of the district attorney and given the mission of specifically targeting corrupt officials and crimes that disrupt the proper function of commerce. Otherwise such crimes will continue to erode public confidence in government and business, and will allow those who prey upon the unsuspecting to go undetected as they pillage the economy and perpetuate misery. Organized crime can continue to flourish, after all, only in a corrupt and compliant society. It relies on a tacit complicity.

THE CARTELS AND THEIR ALLIES

Armed with a clarity of insight born of the repudiation of ideology and coupled with an ethical commitment to enforce the law of the land in an impartial manner, the professional police administrator can lead his or her agency into the fray with a genuine hope of success. Such a leader will readily identify the nature of the enemy that confronts the organization, unencumbered by the blinders of political rhetoric and pseudoscientific marketing. In any case, a police chief will have no say in the policies of correctional officials or those of the many advocacy groups that organize to influence politicians and public opinion. What will matter is the task at hand and the methods that will be used to accomplish it. The wisest course that any chief, sheriff, or agent-in-charge can steer for his or her staff is straight for the goal, no matter the consequence.

This book does not dispute the level of threat that is attributed to organized crime by the law enforcement community. It is grave. Its only dispute is that the police have traditionally failed to pursue such criminals wherever the chase might lead. This must end. The quarry must be given no quarter–no matter how hazardous the field to which it retires. If a money trail should lead a narcotics unit to the doorstep of an old-money pillar of society, there should be no disengagement–there must be no safe zones. It is here that true courage will be tested. It might seem disingenuous for me to assert that there are some things even more frightening than dodging a bullet, but confronting the reality that one's professional career might come to an abrupt and untimely end can have a similar effect. It is an unnerving experience to investigate the powerful, and it is an unsettling realization to learn of their complicity in the trafficking of cocaine or the exploitation of the weak through rackets and prostitution. But there is a great deal of money to be made in the clandestine banking that underwrites the business of the cartels, and there are profits galore in the brokerage of even a single shipment of cocaine. Gambling debts can be wiped away by providing organized crime with the stolen securities it needs to as collateral for foreign loans that underwrite much of its activities. Even local gang leaders need pagers and cars not traceable to a real identity, and someone is there to provide them.

Otherwise legitimate organizations facilitate the activities listed above. Corrupted businesses and compromised public officials provide the avenues of the underground economy through which the traffickers and extortionists of the world conduct their particular brand of commerce. The police must pursue them across the lines of demarcation that have been delineated through the use of power, rhetoric, and fear. Law enforcement must always keep its eyes upon the goal and, when it is thought through, it is a very old and noble goal indeed. Simply put, it is "to catch the bad guys." All any police chief, patrol officer, or special agent need remember is that the "bad guys" do not come dressed only in gang colors or wearing "coke spoon" pendants. They also wear pin-striped suits, and many drive family sedans to work. Not all of them live on the wrong side of the tracks. Far from it–many of them reside in towers on the shore.

The implications of this stance are immediately apparent. Large-scale organized crime and white collar crime units need to be established at the state and local levels and the assets devoted to such matters at the federal level must be increased dramatically. The symbolic efforts of the metropolitan enforcement groups and the greatly underfunded efforts of the federal strike forces and their progeny are to be abandoned in such a plan. What is needed is a well-equipped and well-staffed set of federal agencies when it comes to international smuggling and well-organized criminal enterprises such as the cartels and their domestic counterparts. If it is necessary to double the staff of the FBI, it should be done. If it is necessary to double the fleet of the U.S. Coast Guard, the appropriations should be made. As to the staffing of state and local agencies, much can be accomplished simply be redeploying the resources already in place. It would seem logical to curtail much in the way of services if it means that more will be done to fight crime. There is no disgrace in telling a citizen who has locked his or her keys in the car to call a locksmith instead of the police. Still, more in the way of budget may be needed here also. If so, it should be spent.

NOTES

1. Samuel Walker, *Sense and Nonsense About Crime and Drugs* (Belmont, CA, 1994), 19.

2. Howard Cohen, "Authority: The Limits of Discretion," in *Moral Issues In Policework*, ed. Ferderick A. Elliston and Michael Feldberg, (Totowa, NJ, 1985), 27-42.

3. Ibid., 27.

4. Ibid.

5. Harold F. Gortner, Julianne Mahler, and Jeanne Bell Nicholson, *Organization Therory: A Public Perspective* (Chicago, 1987), 77.

6. Ibid.

7. Ibid.

8. Ibid., 306-307.

9. Jeffrey L. Pressman and Aaron Wildavsky, *Implementation* (Berkeley, CA, 1984).

13

The Cost and the Benefit

At what cost will we achieve the reorganization of America's law enforcement assets? Is the benefit worth the investment? President Clinton has called for 100,000 more peace officers. Congress has called for 50,000. So far as this book is concerned, we would be justified in doubling the system entirely if the need should prove that great. As was revealed in chapter 8, the total budget for state and local law enforcement in the United States runs less than $35 billion. A *U.S. News & World Report* article on the cost of crime in America serves to illustrate just how stingy an investment in the safety of our citizens this actually is when compared with the cost of failure.[1]

In the January 17, 1994 issue of the magazine, the editors of *U. S. News and World Report* put the total price of crime at $674 billion. Of this, they report that $78 billion dollars is spent on the criminal justice system (police, courts, and corrections). Another $64 billion goes to private protection services and equipment. The price put on the loss of life and work is $202 billion, that of crimes against business is $120 billion, and the dollars lost to theft and fraud come to another $60 billion. Drug abuse accounts for another $40 billion in cost to the economy and a staggering $110 billion is forfeited to drunk driving. Figure 13.1 compares these dollar amounts graphically. Even if one extracts the amount of money currently spent on the entire criminal justice system from the overall figure, the staggering sum of $596 billion in costs remains. It would seem obvious that whatever the costs of adding the specialized white-collar/organized crime units at the state and local levels or of properly staffing and equiping those already in existence are trivial in comparison with the

potential benefits. No matter the expense of filling out DEA, FBI, Coast
Guard, and Customs personnel levels and equipment needs, it is preferable to
the alternative. One could double the entire Justice Department budget for less
than 2 percent of the $596 billion figure just cited.

FIGURE 13.1
Costs of Crime in Billions of Dollars

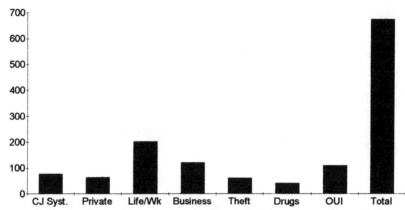

Source: "Violent Crime," *U. S. News & World Report,* January 17, 1994.

It must be conceded that the amount of benefits realized under such a
revamp of the system is unpredictable. I do not know of a way to precisely
calculate the likely savings in terms of dollars, and I am not about to engage in
the contrivance of any such figure. I have no scientific snake oil in stock for
such a deception, nor am I inclined to mine for political or professional capital
with any. Here one must rely on reason and judgment, for some things yet
depend on our ability to intuitively assess the problems that confront us and the
solutions that are offered. Science has limits. It is subordinate to philosophy.
Indeed, once referred to as "natural philosophy," science is but a special brand
of its namesake and, although it is a wonderful tool, it must never be regarded
as a god.

That said, I will assert that whatever the cost of reprioritizing the mission of
law enforcement toward the full intent of the law and to the fullest spirit of the
Constitution, nothing but good can come of it. There were times when
America was much more peaceful than today. There are still places where
children do not need to hide in bathtubs in order to sleep. If the police have
lost their ability to protect our citizens and to allay the fears of our children, it
is because they have lost the ability to fight. And it is not that those who take
the oath and pin on the badge are less courageous than those who have done so

in the past. Far from it. Rather, it is due to the fact, as was noted in chapter 1, that the battle for justice is neverending. Virtue and decadence oppose each other in an ongoing conflict that never ceases, and just as Arthur's knights would invariably fail if ever they lost sight of the virtuous side of their cause, so it is with us in the real world of the modern age. If ideology has blinded virtue and if the politics of bureaucracy has blunted resolve they have done so through deception and a relentless abuse of public discourse. Policework need only reorient its thinking toward its more noble and traditional goal in order to become more effective. It need only rededicate itself to enforcing the law-equally.

NOTE

1. *U. S. News & World Report*, "Violoent Crime," January 17, 1994, 40.

Conclusion: A Return
to Camelot

As one travels down the Kennedy Expressway toward Chicago's Loop, one is always struck by the imposing skyline. It is a trip that I make now on business–I am a civilian again–and it has taught me yet another lesson in life. Just as Dorothy had never really left Kansas, none of us have really left Camelot. And just as surely as the castles of the time of knight-errantry are reincarnated in the skyscrapers of Chicago's Lake Michigan shore, so it is also certain that the hope for justice lives on in the hearts of the citizens of that great city.

Power still reigns from the lofty towers of castles by the shore. Beauty is yet manifested in the artfulness of the architect, even as justice is yet personified in the hearts and hands of the knights of the realm. The nature of the human creature is unlikely to change in the short span of eons. The millennia pass and civilizations rise only to fall, but the soul of the human animal will always be torn between selfish desires and noble causes.

That is why I began this book by stating that the goals of a just society "must ever and more vigorously be pursued." Virtue and decadence do indeed oppose each other in a continuous conflict. It is the same conflict that each of us struggles with, and it gives rise to wars and crime under which each of us must suffer. At the same time, it is the source of inspiration that leads us to create civilizations and the beauty of the arts. It is the destiny of people to struggle and achieve.

Just as we have achieved so much in America, so we are in danger of losing it all. There are many on this planet who point to the modern era of American civilization and assert that it is already in decline. Whether this is certain is a matter to debate. Whether we can continue to thrive as a people and a nation without peace and order is not. Justice cannot take a rest–neither can the keepers of the peace allow it to be set aside.

The police must rise to the occasion if we are to continue the greatest experiment the human race has ever undertaken. Battles are never won by denying the presence of an enemy, and there is no more insidious opponent than the one who hides within our ranks. Do not stand impotent with your weapon in its sheath. The sword of justice serves best when it is wielded. Fight the good fight. Champion the true cause. Stand ready to strike a blow for justice.

Bibliography

Abadinsky, Howard. *The Mafia in America: An Oral History*. New York: Praeger, 1981.

Adler, Patricia A. *Wheeling and Dealing*. New York: Columbia University Press, 1985.

Baber, Walter F. *Organizing the Future*. Birmingham, AL: University of Alabama Press, 1983.

Berger, Peter L., and Berger, Brigitte. *Sociology: A Biographical Approach*. New York: Basic Books, 1972.

Chaiken, Jan; Chaiken, Marcia; and Karchmer, Clifford. *Multijurisdictional Drug Law Enforcement Strategies: Reducing Supply and Demand*. Washington, DC: National Institute of Justice, 1990.

Cohen, Howard. "Authority: The Limits of Discretion." *In Moral Issues in Policework*. Ed. Frederick A. Elliston and Michael Feldberg. Totowa, NJ: Rowman and Allanheld, 1985.

Cohen, Howard and Feldberg, Michael. *Ethics for Law Enforcement Officers*. Boston: National Association of State Directors of Law Enforcement Training, 1983.

Communities Take Action: A Conference Report. Milwaukee, WI: Wisconsin Office of Justice Assistance, 1992.

Conroy, John. *Belfast Diary*. Boston: Beacon Press, 1987.

Crocker, Lawrence P. *Army Officer's Guide*. Harrisburg, PA: Stackpole, 1990.

Cronin, Thomas E.; Cronin, Tania Z.; and Milakovich, Michael E. *U.S. v. Crime in the Streets*. Bloomington: Indiana University Press, 1981.

Drug Enforcement Prosecution in the '90's: A Conference Report. Madison, WI: Office of Justice Assistance, 1992.

Feldberg, Michael. "Gratuities, Corruption and the Democratic Ethos of Policing: The Case of the Free Cup of Coffee." *In Moral Issues in Policework*. Ed. Frederick A. Elliston and Michael Feldberg. Totowa, NJ: Rowman and Allanheld, 1988.

Gortner, Harold F.; Mahler, Julianne; and Nicholson, Jeanne B. *Organization Theory: A Public Perspective*. Chicago: Dorsey Press, 1987.

Gurr, Ted R. *"Historical Trends in Violent Crime: A Critical Review of the Evidence."* In *Violence and Theft*. New York: K. G. Saur, 1992.

Hanaway, Donald J. *The Attorney General's Strategy: Combatting Narcotics in the Nineties.* Madison: Office of the Attorney General of the State of Wisconsin, 1989.

Holden, Matthew Jr. "Imperialism in Bureaucracy." In *Bureaucratic Power in National Policy Making.* Ed. Francis E. Rourke. Boston: Little, Brown, 1986.

The Impact: Organized Crime Today. Washington, DC: President's Commission on Organized Crime, 1986

Kalish, Richard A. *The Psychology of Human Behavior.* Berkeley, CA: Brooks/Cole, 1973.

Lashley, Rickey D. "Limited Centralization of a Metropolitan Enforcement Group: A Case Study." Master's Paper, Department of Urban Studies, University of Wisconsin-Milwaukee, 1991.

Lovell, Rick and Stojkovic, Stan. "Myths, Symbols, and Policymaking in Corrections." In *Criminal Justice Policy Review.* Ed. Robert Mutchnick. Indiana: Indiana University of Pennsylvania, 1987. II. No. 3, 229.

Mack, William P., and Paulsen, Thomas D. *The Naval Officer's Guide.* Annapolis: Naval Institute Press, 1983.

Office of the Comptroller General. *War on Organized Crime Faltering-Federal Strike Forces Not Getting the Job Done.* Washington, DC: U.S. Department of Justice, 1977.

O'Neill, Tip. *Man of the House.* New York: Random House, 1987.

National Drug Control Strategy. Washington, DC: The White House, 1989.

Perrow, Charles. *Complex Organizations.* New York: Random House, 1986.

Pressman, Jeffrey L. and Wildavsky, Aaron. *Implementation.* Berkeley: University of California Press, 1984.

Reiman, Jeffrey. *The Rich Get Richer and the Poor Get Prison.* New York: John Wiley and Sons, 1979.

Report of the National Conference on Organized Crime. Washington, DC: U.S. Department of Justice, 1975.

Report to the Nation on Crime and Justice. Washington, DC: U.S. Department of Justice, 1988.

Sherman, Lawrence W. "Becoming Bent: Moral Careers of Corrupt Policemen." In *Moral Issues in Policework.* Ed. Frederick A. Elliston and Michael Feldberg. Totowa, NJ: Rowman and Allanheld, 1985.

Smith, Dwight C., Jr. "*Ideology and the Ethics of Crime Control.*" *Ethics, Public Policy, and Criminal Justice.* Ed. Frederick Elliston and Norman Bowie. Cambridge, MA: Oegleschlager, Gunn and Hain, 1982.

"Some Call for a Drug Cease Fire." Racine Journal Times, July 11, 1992, 1a.

Uniform Crime Reports. Washington, DC: U.S. Department of Justice, 1971-1991.

U.S. News & World Report. "Violent Crime." January 17, 1994.

Walker, Samuel. *Sense and Nonsense About Crime and Drugs.* Belmont, CA: Wadsworth, 1994.

Warren, Carol A. B. *Sociology: Change and Continuity.* Homewood, IL: Dorsey Press, 1977.

Index

About the Author

RICKEY D. LASHLEY is a claims investigator with CNA Insurance, an adjunct faculty member of the Criminal Justice Program at Mount Senario College, and a former investigator and patrol deputy in Wisconsin. He has written on police matters.

ISBN 0-275-95013-1

90000>

EAN

9 780275 950132

HARDCOVER BAR CODE